What Readers Are Saying A

"Dan Boudreau has done it again! This is ⌐_____
and moving forward with your small busine⌐_____
that not only will you learn from Dan's book, _____ again
for more information and guidance as you ⌐____ your journey through the
world of business."

Allison Nazarian, Owner
Copywriter | Consultant | Internet Marketing Strategist
www.SheWritesMedia.com

"Dan Boudreau has put together an incredible product. The RiskBuster series
provides exceptional user friendly tools packed with valuable information that
offers real life application. I highly recommend the RiskBuster products to anyone
starting a business or growing an existing one. These resources are for serious
entrepreneurs."

David V. Wahlund, President
Manifest Success Projects Inc.
www.manifestsuccess.ca

"RiskBuster is an absolute asset to anyone who needs to create a foolproof business
plan! Without Dan's positive style encouragement & knowledge, I would have
been lost in the process. This book is the foundation for any serious entrepreneur,
hoping to create a true business snapshot. Consider RiskBuster as your business
planning bible, with all the valuable tools you need to guide you to success!"

Angela Bate, Owner
Organic Maid House Cleaning
www.organicmaidhousecleaning.com

"In Riskbuster, Dan Boudreau provides a strategic roadmap for anyone who has
even the slightest desire to start their own business. He covers the good, the bad,
and even the ugly questions that must be asked and answered in order to effectively
plan for a successful business. Tables, checklists, and worksheets included in the
book help anyone get to know the ins and outs of their proposed business from the
ground up. A must read for new (and even experienced) entrepreneurs!"

Suzanne Lieurance, Owner
www.Buildyourbusinesswrite.com

"Riskbuster was written for real people, by a real business person. It's easy to read and easy to follow. The Shell is an amazing tool as it helps you to see what you have, what you need and where you stand in the process. Dan has taken the guesswork out of business planning and provided the tools required to write a strong business plan. When I finished, I had transformed my vision into reality. I am confident in my information and proud to present it.

If you are thinking about starting your own business get this book and get started."

Crystal Prieston, Proprietor
Transform Costumes, Props and Party Supplies
transformpg@shaw.ca

"RiskBuster will definitely help entrepreneurs reach their start-up goals, as well as helping existing businesses to streamline their operations—this is a must have for the small business owner! I believe that this information is more important to the success of a business than the products or services that they sell. I look at it like planning a fishing trip, if you fail to plan ahead to bring a fishing rod, lures, bait, sunscreen etc. your trip may not be successful or very enjoyable. The information provided in RiskBuster helps business owners prepare for challenges that are presented to them so they can have a successful and enjoyable trip in their business ventures. I know it has been a huge part of the success of my business."

Joe Lewis, Owner
Joe-Lewis Fishing Adventures
www.lewisfishingadventures.com

"My experiences with Dan's books have been absolutely fantastic. Not only did they have all the business startup information I was looking for all in one neat package, but they were very user-friendly and easy to follow through step-by-step. I had all the information, and therefore the confidence, to get my business up and running smoothly in no time! I have already recommended Dan's books to others who were starting their business, and I would not hesitate to do so again."

Sarah MacGregor - Your Administration Superhero!
SMac To The Rescue Virtual Administration Solutions
http://www.totherescue.ca

RiskBuster™

Start or Grow
Any Small Business
Wherever You Are With
Whatever You Have
Right Now!

Dan Boudreau

New York

RiskBuster

Start or Grow Any Small Business Wherever You Are With Whatever You Have Right Now!

Copyright © 2009 Dan Boudreau. All rights reserved.

Email orders to **danb@riskbuster.com**

Order online at **www.riskbuster.com**

ISBN 978-1-60037-659-7

Library of Congress Control Number: 2009905159

Cover Design by: 3 Dog Design [www.3dogdesign.net]

MORGAN · JAMES
THE ENTREPRENEURIAL PUBLISHER

Morgan James Publishing, LLC

1225 Franklin Ave., STE 325

Garden City, NY 11530-1693

Toll Free 800-485-4943

www.MorganJamesPublishing.com

Other Books by Dan Boudreau

Business Plan or BUST!

Dedication

This book is dedicated to my sisters, Diane Boudreau, Maxine Koppe, and Jen Higham, and my brother, Larry Boudreau.

Acknowledgments

The first thank you goes to my parents, Clarence and Olga Boudreau, not only for their enduring patience and support throughout my life but because of the entrepreneurial role they have modeled for so many years.

For their friendship, wisdom and unwavering loyalty, I thank Maxine Koppe and Richard Duval.

A special warm thank you goes to Shirly Prokopchuk for her love and support.

I wish to acknowledge and thank Lynette M. Smith for a wonderful and thorough job of editing and formatting. Lavish kudos go to Maxine Koppe and Ray Gerow for a final scouring of the manuscript before sending it off to the publishing team.

I am so grateful to all of those whom I've worked with in the business and economic development field. A heartfelt thank you goes to all of the participants of my business planning workshops for showing me the need for this book and teaching me what needed to go into it.

Thank you to the many readers of my first book, *Business Plan or BUST!*, and to those who took the time to send me feedback.

I wish to acknowledge and thank those who pioneered the *Business Planner's RoadMap*™ and the *RiskBuster Business Planner*™ CD and offered their many suggestions and encouragement.

My sincerest gratitude goes to the team at Morgan James Publishing for their patience and hard work in bringing this book to life. A warm thank you to David Hancock, Rick Frishman, Jim Howard, Sherry Duke, Lyza Poulin, Bethany Marshall and Temeka Shelton—as well as to all others on the team whose efforts have helped to make the publishing process successful.

The list of those who helped bring this book into existence could go on and on. At this writing I estimate that I have had the privilege of serving more than 5,000 learners, either as a coach or in workshops. The development and inspiration for this book has taken place out in the real world, interacting with real people as they plan their small businesses and their futures.

I thank all of those mentioned above and all future readers of this book for the opportunity to share my experience!

Table of Contents

By three methods we may learn wisdom:
First, by reflection, which is noblest;
Second, by imitation, which is easiest; and
Third, by experience, which is the bitterest.

—Confucius

Introduction

Welcome to my world. I've been a small business owner since 1980. My business, Macrolink Action Plans Inc., provides practical, affordable business planning solutions for regular folks with extraordinary business ideas. My business plan is used throughout this book wherever examples are provided.

Until I started my own business, I was a flight risk as an employee. It's not that I didn't enjoy some of the jobs, but inevitably I became dissatisfied and moved on. I can imagine no greater waste of precious life than time spent working at hated or boring jobs, nothing sadder than plodding in to punch a time clock to count the minutes and seconds until the shift ends.

Where we have any influence whatsoever, our lives are to be enjoyed. For those of us who must work, that work will consume more than a third of our time on this planet. Surely there is no greater opportunity to change the flavor of our existence than to take control of our work life, and to work at something we are passionate about. For many people, the best way to do this is to own a business.

From the first moment I stepped onto the business roller coaster, I've been enthralled with it. It is very satisfying to live by your wit, to sustain yourself and your family by doing work you love to do. There are a number of reasons to be excited about owning a business:

- The thrill of shouldering the risk and being 100 percent responsible for your outcomes.

- The potential and anticipation of greater rewards than any hourly job can bring.

- The joy of loving what you do and enjoying your work each day.

In addition, your business can be a platform from which you can make a difference to the world around you. You can build your business to be whatever you want it to be. If you so desire, it can become a vehicle through which you contribute to your community and make the world a better place. That is a whole lot of opportunity!

The primary tool for building a business is the business plan. Had I discovered it sooner, I may have avoided some painful and costly disasters earlier in my business life. The business plan is the ultimate learning opportunity. With the help of this book, you can do it yourself, inexpensively and without putting your investment at great risk.

RiskBuster is a composite of segments from my first book, with a few new articles added where it made sense to do so. Those who have read *Business Plan or BUST!* will recognize the Business Planner's Primer and the Business Planner's RoadMap™. This publication has been shortened to create a less formal, more user-friendly resource for taking a business concept from the idea to opening day.

This book is for anyone who might one day start a business. It is equally helpful for seasoned business owners who have discovered the need for a business plan but have never previously written one. Its ultimate purpose is to make business planning achievable for novices.

RiskBuster can become an indispensible companion throughout the business planning and start-up process. I hope you keep it close during those many hours spent percolating on your business ideas, throughout the start-up process and far beyond as you implement your business dreams to become your reality.

I hope you find many helpful hints in the following pages, and I wish you great success in your business pursuits!

How to Get the Most from This Book

I hope this book is in your hands because you are thinking about starting a business or developing a plan for a business you own.

Here are some suggestions for gleaning the most value, whether you are idly considering a business idea, or serious about getting started:

1. You can quick-read the entire book, playing your business idea through in your mind.

2. You can work through your business concept from start to finish, making notes directly in this book or elsewhere, or perhaps on your computer.

3. The tables and worksheets in the book are downsized to conserve space in this book–they are intended to provide you with the basic idea in order to create your own tables, either on blank paper or on your computer. You can download any of the full-sized tables from the RiskBuster™ website at **www.riskbuster.com/worksheet**.

4. In the RoadMap™, the mini tables just below the title for each step will help you determine whether the step is necessary for your business:

MUST HAVE	RECOMMENDED	NICE TO HAVE

5. You can conduct feasibility studies (see RoadMap™ Steps 11 to 30, pages 65 to 114). These can be informal quick feasibilities, or they can be done with enough structure and vigor to provide a solid foundation for your business plan.

6. You can use this book to develop and write a business plan for any business, small or large, new or already in motion (see RoadMap™ Steps 31 to 99, pages 119 to 286).

The groundwork done in the following pages will enable you not only to build a business plan, it will give you confidence and consistency in your communications with gatekeepers, bankers, employees, partners, and investors. No matter which written documents you decide to produce, the most important benefit will be a measurable confidence in your business idea and your plan.

The Business Planner's Primer

Congratulations for launching on the exciting path to owning your own business! Over the past couple of decades I have coached thousands of people to start their businesses.

Does This Sound a Bit Like You?

- You are excited about your business idea.
- You are afraid of failing.
- You wonder if your product or service will sell.
- You have a limited amount of money to risk.
- You don't want to lose your investment.
- You may be pushed toward business or self-employment out of necessity, or you might be attempting to take advantage of an opportunity.
- You may simply aspire to be your own boss or to create a better lifestyle for yourself and your family.
- You have little or no business planning experience.

If any of the above points describe you, be encouraged. If you really want to start your business, you will do it! Even if this is your first business plan, you will succeed! The planning process can be fun and educational, and it has the added incentive of helping protect your house, your parents' retirement fund, or whatever else you intend to put at risk.

Whether you want to informally research some interesting business ideas or you are eager to roll up your sleeves and develop a business plan, I guarantee the following pages will help, even if you've never previously been in business or written a business plan.

You are launching on an exhilarating learning adventure!

Opportunities Abound

Abundant opportunities drift through our lives at an astonishing rate. Yet many people are victimized by scarcity. Why do some people embrace opportunities and succeed while others do not?

Time fills up with activity. One difference between successful people and the less fortunate is that the successful exert more control over their time. An important part of getting what you want from life is to know what you want, and then invest your time and energy in the activities that bring those rewards to you.

The starting point to filling your time with purposeful action is to know what you want and to have a purpose. If you want to succeed, to achieve your dreams, to experience fulfillment–it will be more efficient to begin with a clear idea of what these things are to you. After all, if you don't know what you're chasing, how will you know if you catch it?

Purposeful action is that which moves you toward fulfilling your vision. If you agree that opportunities are events that can bring you closer to fulfilling your vision, then clarifying your vision is the starting point to selecting the right opportunities for you.

You are an investor poised on the brink of the most important investment of your life–putting your time, energy and money into your own business. Clarifying your personal vision will enable you to choose your opportunities wisely and channel your energy into actions that are right for you.

Link: A Personal Reality Check will help you identify what's important to you. You can download a free Worksheet from **www.riskbuster.com/worksheet/01-personal-reality-check**

The Business of You

You are the most important component to any business successes to grace your future. Here are two powerful tools that I could have used back when I started my first business: the personal strategic plan and personal inspiration lists.

Your Personal Strategic Plan

A Personal Strategic Plan is an amazing tool for getting focused. Reflect on the eight categories and then write out one or more strategic objectives and a couple of goals for each. This can be done in your scrapbook or on your computer. This exercise is intended to help you focus, not mire you in detail.

Physical	Family	Financial	Social
Spiritual	Intellectual	Career	Adventure

Link: Download a free Personal Strategic Plan Worksheet at **www.riskbuster.com/worksheet/02-personal-strategic-plan**

Your Personal Inspiration Lists

Personal Inspiration Lists can help you focus your energy and provide you with a powerful source of motivation any time you feel the need for it. In your scrapbook or on your computer, create lists under the titles below. Be sure to leave some space in each category so you can come back and enter items you think of later. Place the lists somewhere convenient so you can review or add to them as you feel the need.

Strengths	Successes	Areas of Excellence
Dreams	Purpose	Contributions You Wish to Make
Definition of Success		

Link: Download a free Personal Inspiration Worksheet at **www.riskbuster.com/worksheet/03-personal-inspiration**

Taming Your Financial Life

There are a number of things you can do to tidy up a messy personal financial situation. Personal financial management habits cascade into an owner's business like a thundering waterfall. If you have a messy personal financial situation, you may be frustrated that a banker places so much emphasis on your credit record, but it's really not that complicated.

The habits we employ in one situation often spill over into other areas of our lives. The habits we exercise in our personal financials extend into the business financials. It is safe to extrapolate from a war-torn personal financial situation that one will create a similar landscape once in business. You can take a look at your personal net worth and figure it out for yourself. You don't need a banker or a priest to tell you how you will manage your business finances. If you need to change how you manage your financial life, just do it!

Here are seven basic practices to help you achieve the level of financial comfort you desire:

1. Save a portion of your earnings.
2. Control your expenses.
3. Invest your savings to grow.
4. Protect your assets from loss.
5. Make your residence a profitable investment.
6. Ensure a future income.
7. Increase your earning capacity.

The earlier you get started, the sooner you will reap the benefits of your actions.

Link: Download a free Personal Financial Management Strategy Worksheet at **www.riskbuster.com/worksheet/04-personal-financial-management-strategy**

Link: Download a free Owner's Drawings Worksheet at **www.riskbuster.com/worksheet/04-personal-financial-management-strategy**

Why Develop a Business Plan?

There are many sound reasons to create a business plan:

- So you know where you're going.
- To have a roadmap or blueprint for your business.
- To have a document to look back on in order to measure your progress.
- To protect your investment and equity from loss.
- To determine if your idea will work.
- To build confidence in your business.
- To get a loan from a lending agency.
- To access funding from government.
- To reveal and solve problems before starting the business.
- To learn more about your business.
- To create a document you can use to communicate with others, including family, partners, investors, bankers.
- For your own peace of mind.

Do you have other reasons for developing your business plan?

_____

_____

_____

_____

_____

Link: Download a free What's In It For You Worksheet at **www. riskbuster.com/worksheet/06-whats-it-you**

Conquer the Fear of Writing

It's common knowledge that many people fear public speaking, but less well known that lots of people are terrified of writing.

When we speak in front of a group we feel as though we are naked. We expose ourselves to the scrutiny of others. Once we make a mistake we can't take it back; it is immediately visible to our audience and irrevocable. At the core of the fear of public speaking is fear of failure. To many, this fear is limiting. In fact some people never get past the fear, and because of it they vigorously avoid public speaking.

The fear of writing is similar to the fear of public speaking. When we write our thoughts for others to read, we are as exposed as those who stand and speak in front of groups. We open ourselves to be critiqued by those who read our writing, our mistakes forever visible to our audience. Fear of writing stops many people from writing their business plan.

The process of developing your own business plan offers a tremendous opportunity to learn and grow. The skills and knowledge you take away from the experience are forever enriching. Even if you never start the business, you will exit the adventure a wiser, more marketable person.

Here are some pointers to help you along the path:

1. Embrace business planning as a learning adventure.
2. View mistakes as opportunities to learn and to build your business acumen.
3. Seek the opinions and suggestions of others.
4. Be patient and persistent and correct mistakes as they are revealed to you.
5. Get past the fear by just doing it.
6. Start writing your business plan today.

Develop Your Basic Technical Skills

A few years ago it seemed acceptable to elbow your way through the business planning process with a sharp pencil and a calculator. Technology has changed all that. Now it's hard to imagine attempting to create a business plan or operate a business without the use of a computer, email, the Internet, a word processing program, and a spreadsheet program.

A few basic skills in the following areas will make it easier for you to start or grow a business.

1. ***Basic computer skills.*** A decade ago, only 10 percent of my business planning students were computer literate; today more than 90 percent are computer savvy, and almost all own computers. If turning on a computer still causes beads of sweat to form on your brow, and if you're planning to own a business, it's time to bite the technology bullet and learn a few computer skills.

2. ***Email skills.*** This tool has revolutionized business communications. Got a quick question for someone in a different city? Need an efficient way to communicate with your customers? Want to get a research report mailed to you, quickly? Email makes these and many other tasks a lot easier, and if you know how to attach and send files, you will save even more time and energy.

3. ***Internet skills.*** You have an immense global library right at your fingertips. Search engines have become simple enough that you can practically train your ferret to use them. At the time of this writing the US Census population counter indicates more than 6.7 billion people in the world; one click later, another favorite site reveals that more than 1.4 billion of them are now using the Internet, and it's growing!

4. ***Word processing and keyboarding skills.*** You can probably get by without these basic skills in today's environment, but it's bound to be limiting and costly as you hire others to compensate for your lack of expertise. If you're hunting and pecking your way toward owning a business, a tiny investment

in learning basic word processing skills will pay huge and immediate dividends. If you simply wish to improve your typing speed and accuracy, you can download any number of free typing tutor applications from the Web. It seems that most businesses use Microsoft Word™ for word processing, but other applications are available. For example, OpenOffice Suite has a free downloadable option called Writer available at **www. openoffice.org**.

5. ***Spreadsheet skills.*** When it comes to determining whether your business will make money, a spreadsheet will save you a lot of stress. You don't have to know how to create complex formulas or design worksheets in order to enjoy the benefits. All you really need are some navigation skills and a few reliable templates. Most businesses use Microsoft Excel™, but OpenOffice Suite also has a great spreadsheet called Calc.

If you're planning to start or grow a business, or you're simply looking for ways to make yourself more employable in today's job market, these skills are sure to benefit you immediately and over the long term.

Link: Are you ready for business? Download a free Business Readiness Worksheet at **www.riskbuster.com/ worksheet/07-business-readiness**

Tip: A few short years ago, 20 percent of my business planning clients owned computers and many had no computer or Internet skills. Today, almost all clients own computers and 95 percent are skilled at wordprocessing and searching for information on the Internet. The days of doing business without a computer and Internet access are almost gone.

Hitch a Ride on the Shoulders of Giants

A force kicks into play when you get a team of people working together to solve a problem. It's one of the most powerful options we have at our fingertips, and it doesn't have to cost a lot of money.

You can make your business planning easier by organizing a team to help you. It could be as few as three or four respected friends who want you to succeed, or it might involve more.

There are several ways you might enlist others to help. They can:

1. Encourage you and give feedback.

2. Proofread your draft business plan.

3. Help you find people and information.

Your business planning team could include your most respected business minded friends. Choose people who are supportive of your success, who will speak their mind openly, and who have a positive, win-win attitude.

Points to consider when setting up a business planning team:

- Clarify what you want and pitch it clearly.

- Be considerate of the amount of time and energy you request; most of the people you want will be busy.

- Don't enlist people who will cost you a lot of money unless you can afford it.

- Determine in advance what you can do for them; what are the benefits to them for participating on your business planning team?

- Provide prospective team members with your expected timelines. It is easier to get buy-in to a project that has specific targets.

Your willingness to invite others to participate in your business planning process might be a measure of how solidly you believe in your business idea. A lack of initiative or reluctance on your part might be your inner voice signalling to you that not all is right with your idea. You will have to do enough market research to at least gain some confidence in your business idea before beginning to eat up others' time and energy.

You will find a broad range of people to consider involving on your team, including family, friends, a banker, a bookkeeper, a business analyst, a lawyer, suppliers, and customers. It might even include your competitors or someone who is in the same business in a different city or area who doesn't compete with you.

You probably know or know of people in each of the groups listed above. Make a list of those you might wish to include on your business planning team and why. What special skill, attribute, or knowledge can they bring to your planning process? Don't make this process too formal or cumbersome. Keep it simple.

WORKSHEET: BUILDING A BUSINESS PLANNING TEAM	
Prospective team member	
Address and telephone	
Skills and knowledge	
Role team member will play	
Benefits to team member	

Link: Download a free Building a Business Planning Team Worksheet at **www.riskbuster.com/worksheet/08-building-business planning-team**

Prepare to Burn the Midnight Oil

It's the extra mile that usually makes the difference. Any noteworthy achievements in my business have been built over and above the day job, beyond the normal energy outputs and expectations.

Once my training business grew to offer more than 20 courses and workshops, I identified the need for a catalogue. The absence of a catalogue was glaring and the need was pressing, yet there seemed to be no extra hours in the day or night to do the work. I mulled this over for a time, the idea simmering in my mind. One evening I headed home after working all day and got started. After a couple of late nights and early morning stints, I had three-pound bags under my eyes and a draft catalogue. I had "burned the midnight oil" to pull a critical job together.

I have seen this dynamic at work many times throughout my business life. Here are some important points to consider:

- Clarify what you want or need.
- Ask for what you want, and set your goal.
- Know that we can almost always do more than we think we can; it's a choice.
- There is always enough time to do what needs to be done.
- We have access to more energy than we normally think possible.
- When we take the initiative and state our intentions, the universe has an uncanny way of coming onside and bringing the people, the information and the events needed to make our wishes come true.

Many great achievements take place over and above the regular workday. There is always enough time for miracles; it's a matter of identifying the need, developing a plan, and taking action.

Giving Birth to Your Business

As you start planning your venture, it's healthy to separate yourself from your business. From this moment forward, consider your business to be a separate entity from yourself.

What does this mean?

A little investment of energy at this point can pay off later in the life of your business. For example, you should set up a business bank account, rather than mixing your business expenses with your personal. Your accountant and bookkeeper will both be thankful. You will also enjoy the benefits: less confusion and lower accounting and bookkeeping costs.

I have observed many new and experienced business owners who intertwine their business in their personal lives. I have done this in the past, and it only leads to difficulty.

It may help if you think of your new business as a separate entity, like having a baby, building a house, or hatching an egg.

Here are some ways to separate your business from your personal life:

- Separate your personal time from your business time.
- Train your customers to contact you during business hours.
- Remind your friends to contact you during personal hours.
- Open a separate bank account for the business.
- Establish separate telephone and fax numbers for the business.
- Whether home-based or not, create a separate space for the business.
- For a home-based business, have a separate entrance for customers.
- Create a separate Internet and email presence for the business.
- Even if your business is a proprietorship for which the tax authorities view you and your business as the same entity, set up your business with its own bookkeeping and accounting systems.

- Consider yourself to be an employee of your business. Pay yourself a wage, a regular paycheck, if possible (this is sometimes referred to as "Owner's Drawings" or an "Owner's Draw").

- Pay your personal expenses out of your wages, and pay business expenses from your business account.

There are some wonderful payoffs for keeping your personal and business affairs separate. You will:

- Know your personal and business expenses.

- Find it easier to set effective prices.

- Find it easier to deal with auditors.

- Lower your bookkeeping and accounting costs.

- Be better prepared if you decide to sell the business or bring in a partner.

- Have more peace of mind.

Knowing you have much to gain and little to lose, I urge you, at the start of your business planning process, to consider your business to be a separate entity from yourself.

Link: Download your free bonus copy of the RiskBuster Business Planner™ at **www.riskbuster.com/RiskBusterBook**

Tip: Separate your business finances from your personal finances. This will enable you to accurately identify your business expenses, which will make a big difference when it comes to sharpening your pencil to compete for jobs. Don't muddy your business financials with personal expenses.

Myths About Owning a Business

Successful business owners make running a business look easy. Observing from the outside, it's easy to imagine that they harvest massive rewards with little or no effort. That is just one of many misconceptions about owning your own business. Here are a few more:

1. **A business is a get-rich-quick scheme.** It is more accurate to say that most overnight successes take at least 25 years of hard labor. An entrepreneur is a twisted individual who will work 15-hour days at minimum wage to avoid taking a real job at $20 per hour.

2. **Bigger is better.** Be careful what you ask for. The sweet little enterprise you grow might become a treadmill trap, just like the drudgery you attempted to shed by leaving your old job. Millions of small and micro businesses survive and thrive and meet all the owner's needs without growing into large companies.

3. **Most people are *not* suited to own and operate their own business.** I don't buy this. I believe most people *are* suited to own and operate their own business. It's just that many folks never get to the point where they realize they can do it and take the leap of faith!

4. **You need to get into a business you know.** Most people will change careers three to five times during their work life. It's never easy to shift from one career to another, but folks are doing it all the time. Getting into a different type of business has all the challenge and thrill of changing careers, and even more risk. As a business start-up you will find it difficult to get others (bankers, lending agencies) to buy into your entrepreneurial career shift. If you're leaping into unfamiliar waters, you had best be prepared to finance your own adventure.

5. **You need a lot of money to start a business.** While it's true that some types of business have a high start-up price tag, many do not. As a tradesperson who owns all the necessary tools to work for someone else, you probably already have most of what you need to start your own business.

6. **Owning your business is easier than working for someone else.** If you view business owners as being on Easy Street, you are probably missing part of the picture. Most business owners work long hours and endure a great deal of stress to earn any rewards they get.

7. **"Kicking your boss's butt" is a valid reason to start a business.** First of all, that boss is in business because customers pay for the company's products or services. Secondly, kicking the boss's butt will never be enough of a reward to warrant owning a business. You had best dig a bit deeper and get into a business you are passionate about.

8. **Someone needs to lose in order for you to win.** Occasionally I encounter folks who believe they win at the expense of others. This is 180 degrees off the real reason to get into business: to serve. In my opinion, the only real win is when all stakeholders win, including owners, investors, employees, and customers.

9. **Existing revenue sources abruptly stop and you suddenly begin depending on your business.** I equate business start-up to weaving threads together to form a fabric. Those successful owners earning six-digit incomes didn't start out drawing a huge salary from the business. More likely, they held a part-time job or depended on a trusted spouse to pay the bills while the business built its base. While it's true there is a magical day called opening day, you will be weaving the threads of your business fabric long before and long after opening day.

Tip: The best business plans are succinct. It takes more effort to write clearly and concisely. Don't fall into the trap of thinking a thicker wad of paper is going to impress anyone. It's a busy world and readers of your business plan will be grateful for every effort you make to be brief.

Tackle Your Deal Breakers

Some things will stop your business idea, no matter how wonderful it is. These are the costly rough spots that you would rather conceal from the business analyst or banker. Your best strategy is to get any deal breakers onto the table and fix them. In case any of these apply to you, here they are:

1. **100% financing.** Sure, you and I have heard about those folks who manage to get it. It doesn't happen that often; more often it's a deal breaker. Would you invest your savings in someone who apparently doesn't have the will or the capacity to invest in the business personally?

2. **Bad attitude.** Entire books are written on this topic. The real difficulty with this deal breaker is that most polite folks will not tell you that your attitude stinks, instead they will quietly take their business elsewhere. It's not the responsibility of bankers, employees, or customers to create our approach to others. We are each responsible to manage our own attitude.

3. **Cards and toys.** Nasty credit card balances and a yard full of unnecessary toys are indicators. It's not a sin to own toys; it's the high-interest loans with outstanding balances and endless minimum payments that break the deal.

4. **Fantasy forecasts, unrealistic cash flow.** Would you invest your hard-earned savings in a person who can't take the time and effort to build realistic sales forecasts? The cash flow is your opportunity to impress upon the lender that your know your business. It's got to make sense. Missing or inaccurate expenses will destroy the reader's confidence in your projections.

5. **Getting into a business you know nothing about.** If you are asking a lender to finance you to get into a business you know nothing about, be prepared for the jaundiced eye. Many folks have changed careers or leapt into a business they didn't know anything about. I've done it, but at my own risk. Would you have financed me to get into a business I knew nothing about?

6. **Inconsistencies or dishonesty.** Would you invest your money in someone who either doesn't know the truth or doesn't make the effort to tell the truth?

7. **Looming liabilities.** There's nothing quite like a pending legal action or a recent bitter marital break-up to scare off your potential lender.

8. **Not fitting the lenders' priorities.** Lending agencies have different and continually changing priorities. Know what those priorities are, and target the right agency for your type of business.

9. **Outstanding taxes or aging accounts payable.** If your business hasn't been able to pay its bills, you had better have a good explanation why and a bulletproof plan for recovery and success. Specifically, you need to show that you can and will pay back the loan.

10. **Overpaying to purchase a business.** Your inability to negotiate a reasonable price to buy the business raises questions about your ability to survive once in business. With your credibility in question, the deal is broken.

11. **Security doesn't match level of risk.** Are you asking a bank to lend you money with no security? Sorry, banks are not in the business of taking major risks.

12. **Low credit rating.** If you're asking a lender or investor to finance a deal, your credit rating needs to be strong. If your credit history reveals a financial trail of terror, the deal is already broken.

Buy, Build or Franchise

The three main ways for getting into business are to start from scratch, buy a franchise, or buy an existing business. Here are some of the advantages and disadvantages of the three methods.

Starting Your Own Business

Advantages

- More freedom and flexibility in how you design and do things.
- You have control over costs and prices.
- You can usually start and build your own business at a lower financial cost.
- As the owner and designer of your business, you will have complete authority and flexibility to adapt the business to suit your lifestyle and needs.
- You reap all of the rewards for your efforts.

Disadvantages

- You are responsible for developing standards, defining roles, training, managing, and mopping floors.
- Isolation can be an issue.
- You will expend more energy because of the need to develop everything from scratch.
- New businesses have a high failure rate.
- As a lone purchaser, you will pay premium rates for goods and services.
- You take all the risk and blame if things go wrong.
- You are responsible to build your own business plan.

Buying a Franchise

Advantages

- With a reputable franchiser, you will be purchasing a proven business model.

- Standards, roles and training are pre-developed and provided.

- The franchiser provides ongoing support.

- You can benefit from a franchisor's marketing, common branding and customer recognition.

- A good franchisor will make your sourcing easier, and you should benefit from group or bulk buying strategies.

- A reputable franchisor should be able to provide you with most of the raw material for your business plan.

- Franchising is closely regulated, which should make it easier for you to assess the track record and credibility.

Disadvantages

- In many cases you will pay a costly upfront fee to purchase a local franchise.

- In most cases you will have to pay ongoing monthly royalties and fees to the franchiser.

- The franchisor will control your expansion.

- The franchisor will determine and limit the size of your territory.

- For the most part you will be locked into a franchisor's methods, timelines, and processes. You may not have the necessary freedom to adapt to changes.

Links: A search using any of the popular search engines will quickly bring you information on a variety of franchise opportunities. Here are a couple of links to get you started.
The International Franchise Association at **www.franchise.org**
And the Canadian Franchise Association at **www.cfa.ca**

Buying an Existing Business
Advantages

- You should be able to negotiate the price.
- You might purchase the solutions to some of the problems of starting a business.
- If the business model is well designed and working, you may benefit.
- You might benefit from goodwill, that is customer loyalty or traffic and cash flow.
- You might be able to interview existing customers and vendors to gain perspective in your buying decision.
- The existing business should be able to provide at least 3 years' financial history.
- Existing employees and infrastructure could make your entry easier and faster.

Disadvantages

- You could inherit negative results of past actions (unpaid bills, back taxes, lawsuits).
- Negative history with customers could follow you.
- Most lending institutions will not recognize goodwill as a financial value.
- In many cases the goodwill follows the original owner(s).
- Where purchasing the assets of a business, you might inherit faulty equipment or surprise repair bills.
- Unless the existing business already has a business plan, you will be responsible to develop your own.

Name Your Business

Naming your business can be both exciting and agonizing. It is exciting because the naming makes the business a bit more real. It can be agonizing because you want to get it right.

There are legal considerations when it comes to naming your business. You don't want to infringe on someone else's turf by using an existing business name, nor do you want someone else using your business name.

Until you achieve a high degree of brand recognition, your business name should indicate what your business does.

I view the name as having three important components: the grabber, the descriptor and the legal identifier. For example, my business is named Macrolink Action Plans Inc.

The Grabber–I begin with a word I like, "Macrolink," chosen because, to me, pleasant and positive connotations arise from this word and it says something about the image I wish to create.

The Descriptor–"Action Plans" describes the service offered by the company.

The Legal Identifier–"Inc." conveys that the business is registered as a corporation.

Before naming your business, determine what business vehicles are available in your jurisdiction. A business vehicle is also referred to as the form or legal structure. For example, Macrolink Action Plans Inc. is a corporation registered in the Province of British Columbia. Most regions or countries have a range of business vehicles that must be used when conducting business in that locale. In Canada, the proprietorship is the simplest and least expensive form, while the corporation is more complex and more costly to set up and maintain.

Tips for Choosing a Business Name

1. Use Internet search engines to determine if the name is already being used. Plug your name ideas into any of the popular search engines and see what comes up. Too many hits might mean the name is overused.

2. Visit the domain registration websites and determine if the domains are available, using the search function built into the domain registry website. The search results will tell you whether your name is available in the .com, .net, .org, .biz or .info versions–some of the registry sites will also list a number of suggestions close or related to your name.

3. Keep the name as brief as possible. Throughout the life of your business, you and others will write, type, think or speak your business name many, many times. If you wish to inspire others to repeat your business name, make it easy for them to do so. The worst names are typically impossible to pronounce, or they employ so many words that you need an acronym to shorten them. Brief is better.

4. Search copyrights and trademarks to determine if some corporate giant has already secured the name. You can either hire a trademark lawyer to do this or you can do it yourself by visiting the appropriate government agency or website.

5. Bounce the name off others and ask for feedback. How does the name fit the business you are attempting to name? What do they think of when they hear the name? Does the name sound right for the image you wish to portray? Do they know of any other business with a similar name?

Once you have chosen your name, have the appropriate authorities do the necessary search and then register the name in the jurisdiction within which you intend to operate your business.

Link: Want to find out if a potential name is already in use? Here are a couple of ideas that don't take a lot of time. First, do a quick search using any of the popular search engines listed at **www.riskbuster.com/member/market-research-springboard** and then click on any of the domain registry links and do a search to see if the domain is available.

Use the Internet to Research

The Internet has brought the world of market research to our fingertips. Yet unless you know at least some of the basics of how to research, it can be a frustrating experience. The following is an introduction to searching for information using the Internet.

Locating an Existing Business on the Web

Sometimes the easiest way to locate a business is to try guessing its URL and then doing a search for it using your favorite search engine. The URL, or Uniform Resource Locator, is the address of a resource or file on the Internet. An easy way to do this is to write the name of the company–or a series of words you're sure of–in the search box. If you have trouble locating the business, using different search engines may bring different results.

1. Think of the name of the organization you wish to locate.

2. Often you can locate the website simply by using the full business name and doing a search.

3. Another approach is to precede the business name with *www.* and to follow it with the most appropriate top-level domain, such as *.com, .net* or *.org,* for example, **www.riskbuster.com**.

Here are the most common top-level domains:

.com is for commercial websites.

.net is for networks, but can be used by anyone.

.edu is for higher education.

.org is for organizations, often used by non-profits but can be used by anyone.

.biz is for businesses.

.coop is for cooperatives.

.info is open for anyone.

.name is for personal pages.

Many other domains exist, such as those for each country, province or state throughout the world. For a more complete listing, do a search using the phrase "list of domains."

Doing Simple Keyword Searches

It is possible to get results by searching single words using most of the common search engines. Adding more words can help to narrow the search and bring more targeted results. When using multiple words, place the most unique words first.

1. Using phrases can be an effective way of searching. When searching for phrases (using quotations), it is important to understand that the combination of words must be in the correct order. If you're not getting results, try switching the order of the phrase to see what comes up.

2. Use AND or the plus sign (+) to add words. For example, a search for suppliers can be made more specific by adding the area or the type of suppliers you are looking for. Instead of searching for suppliers you could try suppliers AND clothing or suppliers + clothing.

3. Use NOT or the minus sign (–) to subtract words. For example, suppliers NOT turtles or suppliers – turtles.

4. Use OR to broaden your search (OR = more). For example, cats OR dogs.

Almost all portals and search engines will do phrase searching, identified by using double quotes at each end of the phase - "I am a phrase". It's important to know that quotes are used to search for exact phrases only.

The best way to get familiar with searching is to get on the Internet and play. Try different searches, words, and search engines to learn how information is stored and managed. For more detailed information do a word search for "Boolean" or visit these sites:

library.albany.edu/Internet/boolean.html

library.albany.edu/Internet/choose.html

For example, here are some ways to narrow a search for suppliers.

> Add more words: suppliers clothing
>
> Use an exact-phrase search: "Canadian clothing suppliers"
>
> Use the AND (+): suppliers + clothing + Canada
>
> Use the NOT (-) to exclude: suppliers – distributors
>
> Use the AND (+) to add and the NOT (-) to exclude: suppliers + clothing – distributors.
>
> Use the OR to broaden your search: suppliers OR manufacturers + clothing

Where to Search for Information

Search Engines: Indexing the words on every page in their database, a search engine covers Web pages and can include billions of pages. Different search engines can bring different results.

Portals: Offer search, directory, and many other general services such as email, free home page building, news and popular topics. Yahoo!, AOL, and MSN are popular portals.

Directories: A subject directory includes selected websites and classifies them into hierarchical subject categories. Most portals have one, and some specialized directories are available by themselves. They do not index every word on every page.

Newsgroups: Discussion forums organized around a particular interest, issue or activity. They can be used to share expertise, views and information, and to debate issues. Newsgroups can be a great source of technical information.

Archives: Dated information or even complete websites can be accessed through sites such at **www.faqs.org** or **www.archive.org**.

Message Boards: www.boardreader.com reads forums and message boards from more than 750,000 sites.

Blogs: A short form for weblogs, these are personal journals published on the Web. Blogs often include philosophical reflections, opinions on a broad range of issues, and they provide a log of the author's favorite web links. Blogs are usually presented in journal style with a new entry each day.

E-zines: Sites such as LISTZ at **www.tile.net** host many e-zines, mailing lists and related information.

RSS Feeds: RSS is an abbreviation for *Really Simple Syndication*. It is a family of Web feed formats used to publish frequently updated works–such as blog entries, news headlines, audio, and video–in a standardized format.

Researching Business Ideas

Here are some of the free research tools that are easily accessible on the Internet, and which are certain to make your market research easy, fast and fruitful.

About: Visit **www.about.com** to explore this amazing website, which offers articles by more than 750 experts on a range of subjects. It's useful for finding information on different topics and has a handy "See What's Hot Now" link where you can learn which questions and topics are getting the most hits.

Ebay Keywords: Click on **http://buy.ebay.com/index_A-1** to discover a list of the most popular keyword searches at Ebay. This tool helps identify how buyers are finding what they want or need.

Google Trends: Housed at **www.google.com/trends**, this service enables you to plug in keywords or topics and instantly pull up charts and graphs showing broad search patterns and links to the relevant websites and articles that drive them.

Google Insights: This site at **www.google.com/insights/search/#** enables you to search terms and topics and filter by country, region and timeframes. It produces a map showing the regional hot spots for your topic, as well as lists of related search terms.

Google Groups: At **http://groups.google.com** you can search through existing group discussion forums or easily set up your own groups for topics of your choice.

MediaFinder: This website claims to be the world's largest database of U.S. and Canadian magazines, catalogues, newspapers, newsletters and journals. Click on **www.mediafinder.com** and use the keyword search box to locate media for topics you wish to research.

Yahoo Answers: At **http://answers.yahoo.com** you can find out what questions are being asked for a range of categories, along with answers provided by random contributors. You can also ask your own questions and provide answers to others' questions, making this an opportunity to network and be recognized as an expert in any given area.

These tools will strengthen any market researcher's toolchest, and they can be easily accessed at **www.riskbuster.com/member/market-research-springboard.**

Here are a few links to get you started on your market research.

WEBSITE ADDRESSES	
Search Engines	**Domain Registry Sites**
www.google.ca	www.domaindirect.com
www.alltheweb.com	www.internic.net
www.hotbot.com	www.register.com
www.altavista.com	http://domains.yahoo.com
www.dogpile.com	http://allwhois.com
www.search.com	www.newregistrars.com
www.lycos.com	
www.excite.com	**Census Information**
www.yahoo.com	www.statcan.ca
www.mamma.com	www.census.gov
www.gigablast.com	www.census.gov/main/
www.clusty.com	www/popcloc.html

Link: To gain instant access to a variety of market research links, visit the RiskBuster Market Research SpringBoard at **www. riskbuster.com/member/market-research-springboard**

Tip: The preceding links and those that follow are mere drops in the huge well of knowledge that comprises the Internet. You can quickly and easily expand your list of links by searching any topic. Each search engine may bring different results. Currently, my preferred tools are Google™ and Clusty™. Experiment with different search engines to discover which you prefer.

Researching the Internet

www.rbbi.com/links/sengine.htm for a list of truly useful search
engines and tools

www.northernlight.com to do in-depth searches of special
publications

www.completerss.com to search and subscribe to thousands of
RSS feeds, on a variety of topics

http://groups-beta.google.com to search Google newsgroups

www.faqs.org/faqs to search archived Internet FAQs, A to Z

http://netscan.research.microsoft.com/static to search thousands
of newsgroups

www.boardreader.com to search bulletin boards with the
Vivisímo clustering engine
http://websearch.about.com to research just about anything;
expert articles on A to Z topics

http://websearch.about.com/od/searchingtheweb to learn about
searching on the Web

http://tile.net to search email newsletters, e-zines, newsgroups,
vendors, Web articles

www.lsoft.com/lists/listref.html for the official catalogue of
LISTSERV lists

http://mb30.mb.scd.yahoo.com/yahoo to search Yahoo message
boards

www.archive.org/web/web.php to search 40 billion archived
Web pages from 1996 forward

www.researchinfo.com for a market researcher's goldmine

International Research Links

www.fita.org is the source for trade leads, news and events and over 7,000 International sites

library.uncc.edu/display/?dept=reference&format =open&page=68 is VIBES (Virtual International Business and Economic Sources), with over 1,600 international business and economic links

http://170.110.104.75/adsearch.cfm?search_type=int&loadnav=no has country reports by Industry

www.ita.doc.gov/td/tic has USA Dept of Commerce market information for countries and industries

www.jetro.go.jp is the Japanese External Trade Organization

http://projectvisa.com has links to embassies around the world

http://globaledge.msu.edu/ibrd/ibrd.asp accesses international business links

www.tradeport.org/countries offers market reports by country

www.hkecic.com/eng/flash_home.html consists of profiles by the Hong Kong Export Credit Insurance Corporation of the credit and sales situation for many major industries

www.tpage.com is a major source of import/export leads

www.euromonitor.com provides international consumer product market research by Industry

http://us.yesasia.com/en/index.aspx shows pop culture, books, magazines and food of Japan, Korea and China

---

Link: The preceding links are available at the RiskBuster™ website. Go to **www.riskbuster.com/member/market-research-springboard**

Credit and Financing Options

Sources of Financing

The most common sources of money to finance a business are personal contacts, i.e., friends, family, inheritance, mortgage extensions, etc. You should be aware that personal relationships can be jeopardized unless you set the loan up on a business basis, appropriately secured with a principle repayment schedule.

If sufficient financing is not available through personal contacts, you will need to consider commercial lending sources.

Short-Term Financing

MATCHING SOURCES TO SHORT-TERM FINANCING	
· Sources	*Type of Financing*
Chartered Banks, Credit Unions	▪ Accounts receivable ▪ Operating loan ▪ Government guaranteed loan
Trade Credit	▪ Usually 15 to 30 days granted by suppliers before payment is due
Factoring Companies	▪ Buy accounts receivable outright without recourse and assume all risks of collection; will advance funds against purchased receivables, less a percentage
Commercial Finance Companies	▪ Funds advanced upon assignment of receivables and warehouse receipts ▪ Equipment financing

Long-Term Financing

<table>
<tr><td colspan="2" align="center">MATCHING SOURCES TO
LONG-TERM FINANCING</td></tr>
<tr><td align="center">Sources</td><td align="center">Type Of Financing</td></tr>
<tr>
<td>Developmental Lending Agencies</td>
<td>

- Start-up financing
- Upgrading or expansion
- Fixed-asset acquisitions
- Equity financing
- Refinancing
- Change of ownership
- Working capital

</td>
</tr>
<tr>
<td>Commercial Banks</td>
<td>

- Capital financing
- Fixed assets and equipment

</td>
</tr>
<tr>
<td>Sales Finance Companies</td>
<td>

- Purchase of equipment and machinery
- Sales and lease-back options on equipment

</td>
</tr>
<tr>
<td>Insurance and Trust Companies</td>
<td>

- Direct loan secured by fixed-asset mortgage
- Open-market loan by offering debt security on market

</td>
</tr>
<tr>
<td>Government Funded or Guaranteed Loans (usually administered by financial institutions)</td>
<td>

- Product research and development
- Pre-commercial and commercial product development
- Development for international markets

</td>
</tr>
</table>

Types of Short-Term Credit

The following table lists a number of different credit possibilities and interest rate categories. Also listed are the ease of obtaining and the popularity, from the very small business start-up perspective.

TYPES OF SHORT-TERM CREDIT			
Type of Credit	*Ease of Obtaining*	*Interest Rate*	*Popularity*
Advance Sales	Difficult	Medium	Medium
Angel	Difficult	High	Low
Bank Loan	Easy	Low	High
Credit Card	Easy	High	High
Factoring	Easy	High	Low
Government Agencies	Difficult	Low–Medium	Low
Industrial Bank Loans	Difficult	High	Low
Insurance Policies	Easy	Low–Medium	Low
Inventory Loans	Easy	Medium–High	Low
Love Money	Difficult	Low	High
Personal Loans	Difficult	High	High
Promissory Notes	Easy	Medium	High
Trade Credit	Easy	Medium–High	High

Have You Hugged Your Gatekeeper Today?

As you venture down the business planning path, you are sure to encounter one or more gatekeepers. "Gatekeeper" is the term I use to describe bankers, business analysts, and managers of any government programs that might provide funds to your business. While gatekeepers are responsible to protect their employers' assets, they can also hold the key to tremendous opportunity for entrepreneurs.

It is natural for you, as a business newcomer, to be defensive about sharing your business idea with others. I encourage you to rise above your initial apprehension and realize that gatekeepers are continually seeking to invest in well-researched and well-presented businesses. If you've done your homework, you could be offering just the package they are looking for.

Gatekeepers' first order of business will be to perform all the necessary due diligence to determine if your business idea is viable. They will assess whether you can do all those glorious things outlined in your business plan, before taking it forth to run the gauntlet with their boss or the committee that decides whether to lend you the money.

If you are respectful when interacting with gatekeepers they can become tremendous allies in your business planning process. Be thankful for their involvement. Often, they are highly knowledgeable generalists who perform due diligence on a daily basis for a broad range of businesses. They will easily recognize whether you are on or off the rails. If you work with them, they will help you build a stronger business plan.

Working Effectively with a Gatekeeper

1. Be curious. Be a learner. Be coachable!
2. If possible, communicate with the gatekeeper at the beginning of your business planning. Learn the gatekeeper's process and timelines; find out what is expected to be in your business plan, and determine if the gatekeeper wants to give you feedback on your draft business plan.

3. Prepare for your discussions and meetings with the gatekeeper and manage the time efficiently.

4. Know your business plan thoroughly and accept that you may not have all of the answers. If you don't have answers to questions, commit to finding them.

5. Without being a know-it-all, try to anticipate which questions the gatekeeper might ask and have your answers ready. You have two ears and one mouth; listen twice as much as you talk.

6. Be on time for meetings, return phone calls promptly, and honor all promises you make.

7. If the gatekeeper seems to be negative about your business plan, ask why and request more detail until you understand the problem and what you need to do to fix it. Then fix it.

8. If a gatekeeper turns down your application, find out the reason and determine whether the decision is final, or if you can fix the weaknesses and resubmit your plan.

9. Whether you reapply or not, use the gatekeeper's input to strengthen any weaknesses in your business plan.

10. Thank the gatekeeper for the feedback.

Link: Download your free bonus copy of the RiskBuster Business Planner™ at **www.riskbuster.com/RiskBusterBook**

Tip: Gatekeepers who appear to lay roadblocks in front of you are assessing you and your business idea to determine the level of risk. If you meet their requirements, you might just win a supportive friend and the opportunity of your life!

Tips for Writing Your Business Plan

When you are ready to sit down and write, just do it. Some people prefer to write the first draft with a pen or pencil and paper; others are comfortable composing directly into a computer. Choose a method that works for you and a time when you will be left alone without distractions.

The business plan is arranged into a number of small, manageable writing tasks. The following suggestions apply to any of the many steps that include written outputs, as well as to the entire business plan.

With any text Element of your business plan, the first step is to write your rough draft, concentrating on your ideas and all the information you need to include. Don't worry about grammar and spelling or any form of editing in the rough draft; you can polish and add refinements during the revision process. This first draft is not the place to be concerned with perfection.

Read the following list of suggestions prior to writing your business plan. You might also consider copying this list and hanging it in a visible location wherever you will do your writing.

1. **Write in the third person**
   Write about your business and yourself as though they are separate entities. Rather than stating, "I/we expect to bring in $24,000 in sales," you might write, "The business will achieve $24,000 in sales."

2. **Lead your reader from general to specific**
   Make it easy for your reader to understand what you wish to communicate. This general-to-specific suggestion applies to paragraphs, Elements and Sections.

3. **Be thorough**
   Make sure you have included all the necessary information. Check your notes to ensure you have covered all of the important points. Provide answers for obvious questions. Be sure to cover all of the relevant Elements of the business plan and the key points indicated in each Element. In the Appendices, provide any complex or detailed backup information to support the statements in the body of your business plan.

4. **Maintain accuracy**
Can you back up your statements with facts? When you quote text or statistics, ensure that you record them accurately. Look for contradictions that may leave your reader wondering. Accuracy is the foundation that enables your reader to build trust in you and your plan; contradictions and inconsistencies are the seeds that grow into doubt.

5. **Be consistent with names and terminology**
To achieve clear meaning in your writing, choose and use your terms carefully. If you wish to make your writing more interesting by varying your terminology, be sure to provide explanations where it makes sense to do so.

6. **Use an active voice**
Always use the active voice unless there is a good reason to use the passive. Active voice is more direct, more forceful and often easier for the reader to understand. For example, "The owner will contact the customers" is active voice. "The customers will be contacted by the owner" is passive voice.

7. **Write positively**
Wherever possible, avoid writing negative statements, unless the negative aspect of the statement needs to be emphasized. It is advisable to extol the benefits of your products and services but highly distasteful to make negative comments about your competitors.

8. **Minimize jargon**
Jargon is language that fails to communicate because it is full of long or fancy words. Most often jargon takes the form of technical terminology or characteristic idiom of a special activity or group. If you use too many words and expressions unique to your Industry or business, you might confuse your reader. If you need to use jargon, provide an explanation for your reader.

9. **Be concise**
Make all the words, sentences, and paragraphs count by eliminating unnecessary words and phrases. Avoid repeating the same idea using different wording–this tends to tell the reader you are unsure of what you are trying to say. Be careful

to remove every word, phrase, clause, or sentence you can without sacrificing clarity.

10. Avoid clichés

Clichés are timeworn expressions or ideas, such as "the price is right." At best, clichés are obviously borrowed phrases that can be confusing to readers from other cultures. They tend to irritate readers when used repeatedly.

11. Choose the right words

Avoid double-edged words—words that can carry an undesired connotation. Also vague or pretentious words, coined words and unnecessary intensifiers should be replaced or deleted.

12. Eliminate awkwardness

Awkward writing can make it more difficult for the reader to understand your message. To smooth your writing, keep the sentences uncomplicated and eliminate excess words.

13. Correct all typos and grammar errors

The errors that result from carelessness have a tendency to stand out to a reader and sabotage the reader's confidence in the writer's ability. Scour your document for the obvious embarrassing errors like misspelled words and missing commas. It is wise to have someone proof the plan for you.

14. Create a visual format that is easy to read

Use a mixture of text, tables and bulleted lists. Keep your paragraphs short to break text into smaller bites and make it easier to read.

15. Use appropriate pictures and diagrams

Use pictures or diagrams only where they complement or simplify your message. Avoid using eye candy simply to impress your reader, unless your business plan is for a graphics-related business. Overuse of pictures can dilute your message and create the impression that you're not serious.

16. Include your sources for key information

If you use tables from the local census archives, state the source. If you quote an article from a credible trade magazine, provide the name of the magazine and the article, as well as the date.

This helps the reader build credibility and confidence in your research and your business plan.

17. Include important detail in the Appendices

Whereas it is important to include a brief biography in the body of your business plan, it is more appropriate to house your complete resumé in the Appendices.

18. Refer the reader to related information

For example, at the end of your biography you might state, "See complete resumé in Appendix F."

19. Ensure numerical information matches text statements

A common mistake in business plans is to state conflicting information in different Sections or Elements of the business plan. For example, stating a different sales total in the Executive Summary than that shown in the Financial Section. Go through your plan and double check for this kind of discrepancy–before it gets into the hands of your reader.

20. Build a complete and cohesive communication package

As a business planning coach, I often write up a list of questions and comments for a business planner. Invariably, the writer of the plan then responds with a list of answers to my questions. Over the duration of the business plan development, we sometimes do this half a dozen times or more, resulting in a half-baked business plan and up to four lists of responses filling in the holes. This is the raw material, not the finished product.

A finished business plan is one complete, cohesive communication package, with any important detail attached in the Appendices for reference. Rather than submitting a half-baked plan with a tangle of disjointed responses to others' questions, create a full plan with all the information included.

Link: Would you like to receive business planning tips by email? Learn more about RiskBuster Business Planning Tips by visiting **www.riskbuster.com/letter/business planning-tips**

Make Your Business Plan Easy to Read

Here are a few ways to make your business plan easier to read.

1. Use simpler words where you can.
2. Use short sentences.
3. Use short paragraphs.
4. Break up your text with an appropriate amount of white space.
5. Use **bold** or *italics* to highlight or **draw attention** to words or phrases *where appropriate*.
6. Use bulleted lists.
   - ✓ Did I say–use bullets?
      - o There are a few different kinds of bullets
         - ➢ Keep it simple. Don't use too many different types of bullets.

7. Use numbered lists.
   1. Numbered lists help us read and remember.
   2. Numbered lists can also help us prioritize.
   3. Numbered lists are easy to refer to.
   4. Use numbered lists mixed with bullets.
      - ✓ You can also add an indent for effect.
         a. Sometimes lettered lists work well for detailed sub-lists.

8. Use tables where appropriate.

TABLE EXAMPLE		
I Am a Table	*One Day*	*Ten Days*
Use tables.	1	10
Tables work great for arranging numbers.	+2	+20
They are especially great for totals.	=3	=30
Tables enable us to organize information.	Capital Assets	Small Tools
You can merge cells to form larger cells like this one.		
⇐You can left justify like this.	You can right justify like this.⇒	
You can center ⇔ like this.		
You can use tables with or without borders.	This table has borders.	

9. The text box is another great tool.

> This is a text box. Do I draw your attention?

> A text box can be used to break out, separate or highlight information. It can also be used for lists like this:
>
> Year One Sales = $100,000
> Year Two Sales = $150,000
> Year Three Sales = $200,000

10. Color can be fun, but the more colors you use the more expensive the printing. Some colors are more difficult to see than others.

11. CAPITAL LETTERS can set WORDS or HEADERS apart from other text.

12. You can use different font sizes for functions such as Headers.

13. Some fonts are easier to read, others are difficult to read.

14. For some things, a picture can be worth a thousand words.

15. Graphs are great for showing trends.

16. Pie charts work well to show portions of a whole.

17. Bar graphs are an effective way to show sales.

18. For the tables and summaries in your business plan, round all figures up to the nearest dollar and eliminate any unnecessary zeros and redundant currency signs.

19. Don't overdo it with the "special effects." Keep it clear, simple, and professional.

Link: Subscribe to the RiskBuster™ Newsletter and download a free gift at **www.riskbuster.com**

Dan's Top Business Planning Tricks

1. Do your business plan for yourself first, and then craft it into a tool for communicating to others.

2. Write for your average reader; don't try to baffle your audience with big words or complexity.

3. Champion your own business planning process, don't give away the privilege.

4. Do your own market research–be the expert for your business.

5. Business planning is a confidence-building process; don't miss it by hiring someone to do it all for you.

6. Engage someone you trust as a sounding board to discuss all aspects of your business concept. This is critical in order for you to process your thoughts and ideas.

7. Ensure that the narrative part of your business plan is consistent with the Financial Section.

8. Back up your narrative and financial assertions with supporting information and documentation in the Appendices.

9. Clean up any inaccuracies and inconsistencies yourself, don't leave it to your reader.

10. Be curious; identify and challenge your assumptions.

11. Determine what will prove each Element of your business plan and prove everything you can. Ensure that you use conservative assumptions for aspects you cannot prove.

12. When using assumptions, state them for your reader.

13. Keep the body of your business plan succinct and refer the reader to detail in the Appendices.

14. Forecast sales conservatively low.

15. Estimate expenses aggressively high.

16. Prove your business case. Leave no stone unturned in leading you and your reader to the conclusion that your business can live in the gap between supply (cost) and demand (price). If

you can't prove your business case, start a different business or get a job.

17. Focus on your own strengths and positives rather than the competitors' weaknesses and negatives.

18. Don't prevail upon your reader to go fishing for information. Create one complete and cohesive communication package that is easy for your reader to read and understand.

19. Go as far as you can see, then you will be able to see further.

20. Remember: You are creating a business plan, not building a piano!

Tip: Building a business plan for a proven business concept is very different from creating a new business concept from the ground up. Aspiring business owners can get mired in their attempt to build their product or service offering. You are pioneering, which naturally could lead to a fair bit of trial and error before you settle on a concept that will work. It is natural and acceptable to spin a few circles at this stage before you settle on your opening-day product and service offering.

Get Equipped for Business Planning

Congratulations for recognizing that you need a business plan. If your business idea proves viable and you proceed into business, you are in for one of the most exhilarating adventures of your life!

Your energy will drive this process. You control the amount of time it will take to complete your business plan. The time it takes to get to opening day depends on how much of each day you can invest. You are the boss!

Step 1: Welcome to the RoadMap™

MUST HAVE	RECOMMENDED	NICE TO HAVE

The Transition from Idea to Action

Every business starts with an idea. The idea grows in the mind of the entrepreneur until he or she can no longer ignore it; that's usually when the research process tends to become more formal. Though there are different ways to roll into a business idea, the process of nurturing it into a business plan is similar for many businesses.

- You might love to work with wood and want to create birdhouses for a major chain of stores.

- You may be skilled at a trade and want to provide your service from your home-based shop.

- You might clean houses for busy people or paint wonderful pictures or build a unique line of furniture.

- You may have been laid off by an employer who now wants to hire you as an independent contractor.

- You might be retired and considered unemployable by the employers in your Industry.

- You may have invented a solution to one of the world's major problems and wonder how to get it to the market.

You will know when it's time to research your market. Your business idea will dominate your thoughts; you will be driving those near you crazy with your ramblings. You will be investigating similar products and services and pointing out weaknesses in competitors products. You will be trying to sell your friends on the idea. (Your friends might be encouraging you, or they might just be tired of listening.) There will come a time to get serious about your market research. Only you can decide when that is.

Regardless of your area of pursuit, the dynamics are similar. You percolate on your idea until one day you simply must shift into business planning mode or lose your mind.

Tip: While a business plan will help to increase your knowledge of your business, it will not do much toward helping you develop business trade skills, such as how to handle money, and how to buy, sell, and pay. Business trade skills are more likely to be learned from managing a paper route or operating a lemonade stand. Owning a business is the best way to learn the basic survival skills like knowing how to read the market, how to learn from it and how to change your mind.

Introduction to the Business Plan: Structure and Process

The following table provides you with an introduction to the business plan structure or Shell™. The Shell™ is arranged to be a final presentation for the reader of your business plan, while the RoadMap™ is the step-by-step process you will follow to build your business plan.

The following table provides a snapshot of the Business Plan Shell™. Note there are 6 Sections, 39 Elements, and 24 possible Appendices. The table shows the Elements *in the order in which they will be presented to those who read* your business plan.

Your completed business plan will be made up of three main parts: narrative, financial, and supporting information. Sections 1 to 4 will house the narrative, Section 5 holds the Financial Elements, and Section 6 contains the supporting information.

The business planning process is the 99-step RoadMap™, which blends the market research and business plan writing processes, enabling you to move logically from the first idea through to implementation of your business plan.

THE BUSINESS PLAN SHELL

1. Introduction
  ☐ Title Page
  ☐ Executive Summary
  ☐ Table of Contents
  ☐ Confidentiality and Copyright

2. Business Concept
  ☐ The Business
  ☐ Products and Services
  ☐ The Industry
  ☐ The Owner(s)
  ☐ Strategic Plan and Goals

3. Marketing
  ☐ Market Area
  ☐ Location: Marketing
  ☐ Profile of the Customers
  ☐ Competition and Differentiation
  ☐ Sales and Distribution
  ☐ Servicing and Guarantees
  ☐ Image
  ☐ Advertising and Promotion
  ☐ Pricing Strategy
  ☐ Marketing Action Plan

4. Operations
  ☐ Description of the Operation
  ☐ Equipment and Methods
  ☐ Materials and Supplies
  ☐ Risk and Mitigation
  ☐ Management
  ☐ Professional Services
  ☐ Employees and Contractors
  ☐ Operational Action Plan

THE BUSINESS PLAN SHELL

5. Financial

- ☐ Sales Forecast
- ☐ Explanation of Projections
- ☐ Market Share
- ☐ Cost of Goods Sold
- ☐ Labor Projections
- ☐ Cash Flow Forecast
- ☐ Operating Expenses
- ☐ Projected Income Statement
- ☐ Break-even Analysis
- ☐ Pro Forma Balance Sheet
- ☐ Start-up Expenses
- ☐ Uses and Sources of Funds

6. Appendices

- ☐ Resumé(s)
- ☐ Personal Net Worth Statement(s)
- ☐ Certificates and Accreditation
- ☐ Historical Financial Statements
- ☐ Organizational Charts
- ☐ Board or Band Council Resolution
- ☐ List of References
- ☐ Letters of Reference
- ☐ Letters of Intent
- ☐ Contracts or Offers
- ☐ Partnership Agreement
- ☐ Lease Agreement
- ☐ Insurance Documents
- ☐ Price Lists
- ☐ Price Quotes
- ☐ Appraisals
- ☐ Market Survey Results
- ☐ Map of Area
- ☐ Environmental Information
- ☐ Publicity
- ☐ Promotional Material
- ☐ Product Literature
- ☐ Technical Specifications
- ☐ Glossary of Terms

Step 2: Prepare to Embark

MUST HAVE	RECOMMENDED	NICE TO HAVE

You have begun a journey that will change your world.

You may be starting down this path with no business idea at all, with only an idea for your business, or with a business already in motion. No matter–the RoadMap™ will give you control of your planning process.

Along the way, you may doubt yourself, your business idea or others. You must begin to gather a strong support system for your journey. One key to your success is to keep working toward your vision, regardless of obstacles.

One of the most powerful tools in your toolkit is your written personal vision and goals. There is pure magic in the simple act of writing down what you wish to achieve. You don't always have to be able to see the solutions in order for them to work. When your goal or vision is written, the power of the universe begins to work with you to bring about success. Solutions will gravitate toward you. You will find the right people, knowledge, skills, and information you seek. To prove it to yourself, simply write out your goals and watch miracles blossom before your eyes.

Time Management for the Business Planner

Your business plan will come together more quickly if you invest sufficient time in the process. Of course it will take a lot longer to complete if you're working at a job full-time or have other commitments that tie up your time and energy, but that's acceptable too. The key is to use this process in a timeframe that works for you and your business.

Your business planning will go more quickly if you come to the process having already done part of the work. For example, many people think about their business idea for years–reading, talking, asking, listening, watching relevant videos and reading everything they can. Obviously those who have invested time and energy on their business idea should progress more quickly than those who have never previously given business ownership a thought.

External events may affect parts of your journey. Instead of stressing, keep pushing forward. If any step or task stops or frustrates you, apply your energy to another part of the process. Should you find yourself blocked for any reason–discouragement, disillusionment, procrastination–there's no antidote quite like action. Just keep rolling forward!

From the very beginning, split your time between researching, writing and forecasting. The key is to work on each aspect of your process simultaneously. Here is one example of a daily business planning schedule.

ONE WAY TO ORGANIZE YOUR PLANNING TIME		
Activity	*Estimated Time*	*Tool*
Researching	3 hours	RoadMap™
Writing	2 hours	Shell™
Forecasting	1 hour	Biz4Caster™

Use time allocations that work for you, but keep pressing forward on all three activities until you complete your business plan.

Actions

The RoadMap™ is laid out in 99 logical steps to provide you with a structure to navigate the business planning process. Begin by scanning the entire process to get a sense of how it flows.

It is a matter of following the steps, which consist of one or more bite-sized tasks arranged in an order that enables you to systematically build your plan.

If you have a computer, your business planning process will involve three main tools, the RoadMap™, the Shell™ and the Biz4Caster™. Everything you do in any of the three tools is for the purpose of completing your business plan, which will ultimately end up in the Shell™.

1. Quickly read or scan the RoadMap™.

2. Set up a working copy of your business plan. From the RiskBuster™ CD or download menu, select "Start a New Business Plan" to open a copy of the Business Plan Shell™. Use the File, Save As option to save a working copy of the file onto your computer in which you can begin creating your own business plan. This is the file or document that will house your finished business plan. If you do not have the RiskBuster™ CD, you can download the Business Plan Shell™ free from **www.riskbuster.com**.

3. Set up a working copy of your financial scenario. From the RiskBuster™ CD or download menu, select "Start a New Financial Forecast" to open a copy of the Biz4Caster™. Use the File, Save As option to save a working copy onto your computer in which you can begin building your own financial scenario.

4. Begin working through the RoadMap™ steps, writing narrative in the Shell™ and building your financial scenario in the Biz4Caster™.

Link: Learn more about the RiskBuster Business Planner™ at **www.riskbuster.com/content/riskbuster-digital-business-planner-description**

Link: Download your free bonus copy of the RiskBuster Business Planner™ at **www.riskbuster.com/RiskBusterBook**

Link: Download a Business Planner's RoadMap™ Checklist **www.riskbuster.com/worksheet/66-99-step-roadmap-checklist**

Step 3: Chart Your Path

MUST HAVE	RECOMMENDED	NICE TO HAVE

One thing you can do immediately to lighten your workload is to use technology.

Action

Decide whether you will use low tech, high tech or a combination of the two and gather together the tools you will need to complete your business plan. There are essentially three options for this task.

- **Low Tech:** The low tech path would be to complete the tasks using a couple of lined notebooks, spare paper, a pencil, an eraser and a calculator.

- **High Tech:** This path will require that you prepare yourself with the items listed above and a computer with Microsoft Office™ or equivalent software, a printer, Internet, email capability and the Macrolink RiskBuster™ (including the Shell™, the Biz4Caster™ and sample business plans).

- **Both Low and High Tech:** You may find that you prefer to carry out certain parts of your process using low tech and others using high tech.

Most of your business planning needs will be met by using a word processor, a spreadsheet, and a Web browser. If you don't own these applications, free downloadable open-source options are available that will more than meet your needs.

Application	*Microsoft Office™*	*Open Source*
Word Processor	MS Word™	OpenOffice Writer™
Spreadsheet	MS Excel™	OpenOffice Calc™
Web Browser	Internet Explorer™	Mozilla Firefox™

Step 4: Organize Your Work Space

MUST HAVE	RECOMMENDED	NICE TO HAVE

As you research your market, you will accumulate information, articles, reports, magazines, newspaper clips, and other assorted documents. If you have a computer, you will also gather a lot of the information in digital format.

Actions

Get organized. Create places to store your hard-earned market research information, whether electronic or hard copy.

1. **Determine where you will work.** Determine where to locate your work and storage areas. Physically, this means setting up an efficient work area and figuring out where to store your books and files. Digitally, determine where you will locate your business plan and create a main folder called My Business Planning Project.

2. **Create your hard file storage area.** Set up a place for your business planning project in your file cabinet or file storage box. At a minimum, begin with one folder for your business plan and one for market research documents. Use the categories listed under item three as a starting point for your filing system.

3. **Create your digital business planning folder.** Set up a folder for your business planning project on your computer. At a minimum, begin with one folder for your business plan and one for market research documents. Your list of folders will grow as you begin to develop different Elements of your business plan and Appendices. The following table has some ideas to get you started.

| ORGANIZE YOUR FILE FOLDERS: HARD COPY AND DIGITAL ||
Folder	*Files*
Administrative Files	Action Plan, Vision, Goals, Survey Questionnaire Form(s)
Holding Tank	All homeless clips and files, until you find a home for them
Market Research	Completed Surveys, Research Documents, Clips, Quotes, Tables
Business Plan	Your Business Plan and Financial Projections
Appendices	Use your short-list of Appendices (see Step 11 on page 65)

4. **Set up a binder for market research documents.** Whether or not you gather the market research documents digitally, you may find it easier to read them in hard copy. This is one way to organize the documents so they are easy to locate for reviewing purposes. If you prefer, you can simply store these hard copy printouts in a file folder as indicated previously for the digital counterparts. Depending on how many of this type of document you collect, you may wish to insert a set of tabs to make it easier to source the information.

5. **Organize a bookshelf.** If appropriate, you may also wish to make space available for books related to your business studies and planning.

Step 5: Establish Your Timelines

MUST HAVE	RECOMMENDED	NICE TO HAVE

If you are starting a new business, when do you wish to open? If you are already in business, what date will you implement this plan? If you have a start-up or implementation date in mind, write down your goal.

Action

Identify and write your goals.

WORKSHEET: BUSINESS PLANNING GOALS	
Goal	*Completion*
1. Complete market research.	
2. Complete business plan.	
3. Start business.	
4.	
5.	
6.	
7.	
8.	

If you don't know your start-up date, move on to the following steps and come back to set this goal once you have a clear target in mind.

Link: Download a free Business Planning Goals Worksheet at **www.riskbuster.com/worksheet/09-business-planning-implementation-goals**

Tip: Not writing a goal is the same as not setting a goal; it is one of the ways we deceive ourselves into avoiding the commitment. Write your goals.

55

Step 6: Create Your Action Plan

MUST HAVE	RECOMMENDED	NICE TO HAVE

An action plan is a systematic process for clarifying and targeting your longer term goals and breaking them down into smaller short term goals. You might choose to try using this tool to tackle any one of the goals you set in Step 5 (see page 55). If you don't need this step now, bypass it and come back to it when you see a need for it.

Action

Develop your action plan for success. An action plan includes the following eight steps:

1. Write your goal clearly and in detail.

2. List all the benefits of achieving your goal.

3. Identify the people, information, actions and anything else you need to make your goal happen.

4. Describe the biggest hurdle you need to get over to achieve your goal and how you will overcome it.

5. List those who will support you and what type of support you hope to receive from each one.

6. Set an overall timeline to reach your goal. Break it down into smaller monthly, weekly and daily goals. What will you do tomorrow to bring you closer to your goal?

7. Describe when and how will you reward yourself.

8. Write one or more affirmations that support you in accomplishing your goal. Repeat your affirmations to yourself regularly. Affirmations are positive, easy to remember, and written in the present tense.

Affirmation: I hold a copy of my completed business plan in my hands. I am confident about starting my business because of the great learning experience it has been to develop my own business.

Link: Download a free Action Planning Worksheet from the page at **www.riskbuster.com/worksheet/10-action-planning**

Step 7: Wade Into Your Industry

MUST HAVE	RECOMMENDED	NICE TO HAVE

This activity is intended to help you get immersed in your Industry and your business by subscribing to and reading one or more trade publications, and by researching and joining one or more associations.

How do you benefit by joining trade publications or associations? Here are a few suggestions:

- To learn who the leaders are and what they are doing and saying.
- To identify networking, educational, marketing or advertising opportunities.
- To learn about the Industry or industries affecting your business.
- To keep current on Industry issues, trends and events.
- To discover possible leads or ideas for customers.
- To keep tabs on your competitors.
- To make contact with suppliers or customers.

Actions

The main point of this step is to set out to become an expert on your targeted business and Industry.

1. In a library or on the Internet, search, locate, and read trade publications relevant to your business. If a publication seems appropriate, subscribe to it.

2. Research relevant trade associations. Select at least one suitable association and join it.

Link: Largest database of USA and Canadian magazines, catalogues, newspapers, newsletters, and journals from the site at **www.mediafinder.com**

Step 8: Start a Research Scrapbook or Journal

MUST HAVE	RECOMMENDED	NICE TO HAVE

Your research scrapbook can serve as your trusted companion throughout your planning adventure. It will help you get through the process and provide you with a forum to vent, to store information, and to process your thoughts. Here are some suggestions as to how you might use your scrapbook:

- Write your goals, vision, and mission.
- Record market research information.
- Make lists of things to do and write affirmations.
- Record quotes or clips that inspire you.
- Ask questions (and answer them if you wish).
- Identify problems or challenges and clarify confusing things.
- Whine if things aren't going the way you want!
- Write down what you are experiencing or learning.
- Record sales leads, contact information, and market research.
- Make general notes on conversations or information gathered; write portions of your business plan
- Paste or clip-in business related pictures, articles or information and jot down creative or innovative ideas
- Congratulate yourself on tasks well done.

Action

Start your business scrapbook. Use either a simple lined notepad or purchase a fancier book if that appeals to you. Make it something you will enjoy writing in and using.

Step 9: Write Your Business Vision

MUST HAVE	RECOMMENDED	NICE TO HAVE

I suggest you take some time prior to immersing yourself in market research to write your vision for your business idea.

Allow yourself at least one uninterrupted hour. Find a comfortable spot where you can be creative, think and write. Stick to this process and within an hour you should have a draft vision to use as a benchmark for creating your business plan.

Before you launch, here are a few tips to propel you into "business visioning nirvana":

- Write your vision for some point in the future–pick a date, perhaps your opening day, and write how you wish it to be.
- Don't worry about perfection… keep it simple.
- "Holes lead to goals"; it's helpful to keep a piece of paper handy to write yourself a list of "things to research" for information that doesn't easily find its way into this writing.

Actions

1. Identify your business. (1 paragraph)
2. Develop your mission statement. (1 sentence)
3. Write your vision statement. (1 sentence)
4. Describe your product(s) and service(s). (1 paragraph or table)
5. Describe your Industry trends and the niche your business will serve. (1 paragraph)
6. List your overall business objectives. (3 to 5 points)
7. Describe your customers. (1 paragraph)
8. Describe your major competitors. (1 paragraph or table)
9. Explain why you are qualified to operate your business. (1 paragraph)
10. Outline your financial requirements. (1 sentence)
11. Describe what security you will provide to finance your venture. (1 paragraph)

Step 10: Set Out to Prove Your Business Case

MUST HAVE	RECOMMENDED	NICE TO HAVE

The following Steps 11 through 30 will lead you through the process of researching your business idea. Hopefully, the market research steps will also result in proving your business case. The most common pitfall with business plans is that they do not prove the business case, which is the result of inadequate market research. *This may be the most critical step in the entire business planning process.* It's important enough to take time to understand how to prove your business case.

Civilian Lingo	*Accounting Gibberish*	*Plain Old Numbers*
Demand @ Price	Sales	$128,242
Minus Supply @ Cost	COGS	$ 22,917
Equals Enough Money to Survive and Thrive	Operating Expenses	$ 93,264
	Profit	$ 12,061

If accounting or financial terms cause you stress, use the common terms in column one: demand, supply and enough money for your business to survive and thrive. These terms are more practical for the discussion on proving your business case, because the matter of proof goes beyond financial viability into many areas of market research. The following table provides an idea of what it means to prove your business case.

Link: Download a free Proving Your Business Case Worksheet at **www.riskbuster.com/worksheet/11-ideas-proving-your-business-case**

Link: Download your free bonus copy of the RiskBuster Business Planner™ at **www.riskbuster.com/RiskBusterBook**

Strengthen or Weaken Your Business Case

Here are ways to strengthen or weaken your business case.

STRENGTHEN OR WEAKEN YOUR BUSINESS CASE	
Strengthens Your Business Case Argument	*Weakens Your Business Case Argument*
• Having spoken to real customers.	• Not having spoken to customers.
• Forecasting sales conservatively.	• Making pie-in-the-sky sales forecasts.
• Having signed contracts or letters of intent from customers willing to buy your products or services.	• Having a "build it and they will come" attitude and approach.
• Estimating expenses a little higher than you believe they might be.	• Providing low or incomplete expense projections.
• Demonstrating smart shopping and sourcing.	• Demonstrating lazy or sloppy sourcing; paying too much.
• Being accurate, realistic and truthful throughout your business plan.	• Being inaccurate; using half-truths or false statements of any kind.
• Answering your readers' questions in your plan.	• Leaving your readers with unanswered questions.
• Using clear, believable language.	• Using fuzzy, unclear language of any kind.
• Using accurate, reliable and credible sources for key information.	• Using unknown, inaccurate or unreliable sources of information.

Strengthens Your Business Case Argument	*Weakens Your Business Case Argument*
• Providing clear, accurate references for your sources of information and attaching supporting documentation in the Appendices.	• Leaving your reader wondering where your information comes from.
• Providing a complete set of clear and realistic financial forecasts that you can discuss intelligently with your banker or investor.	• Having financial projections that are too skimpy or too overwhelming.
• Making it easy for your reader to understand.	• Making it difficult for your reader to understand.
• Knowing your business.	• Not knowing your business.
• Knowing your Industry.	• Not knowing your Industry.
• Using common sense.	• Not using common sense.
• Having experience related to your business or Industry.	• Not having experience related to your business or Industry.

Action

Map out how you will prove your business case.

Embrace Market Research

Market research is the process of educating yourself about your business. It includes everything you do to prove or disprove your business case.

The most common reason for failure in business is insufficient market research. Most unsuccessful business plans fail because of weak or ineffective market research. There can be several reasons for this:

- Market research isn't easy.
- For most people, market research is unfamiliar, daunting work.
- The goals of market research are not clear to those who have not previously done it.
- To be effective at researching your market, you have to get out and talk with real people who might not agree with- or challenge your ideas.
- The researching process is a sea of change from start to finish, and change can be frightening.
- You need to multitask, keeping your complete business plan in mind. For example, you might be searching for information on your customers and discover a nugget about your Industry; you need to be able to manage the information effectively.
- Time and life are typically already full to the brim when we start researching.
- Many people give up part way through the market research process.
- One possible outcome is that your business idea is unworkable, which can seem like failure.

Quite naturally, people tend to have a lot of questions when beginning to research their market.

- How much market research is enough?
- Who do I talk to?

- What questions do I ask?
- How do I know when I have proven my business case?
- How do I gather information about my competitors?
- How do I know if people are telling me the truth?

These questions can be daunting, particularly if you have never developed a business plan. Steps 11 through 30 will bring you the answers to these and many other questions.

As you research your market, your confidence in your idea will either increase or decrease. As you ask questions and listen to the answers, you will become very knowledgeable about your business. If your research confirms that your business idea is viable, you will eventually reach a stage where you are confident enough to start your business or implement your plan. If the opposite occurs and you decide not to proceed with your plan, the market research has done its job, which is to save your energy and investment for a different venture.

Market research dovetails into many different parts of your business plan. *By the time you complete your market research process (Step 30), you will have written draft versions of at least three Elements of your business plan.* You will also have revised and rewritten some of those Elements a few times as you learn more about your business idea.

Most importantly, you should be well on your way to becoming confident in your ability to make your business successful.

Step 11: Set Up Your List of Appendices

MUST HAVE	RECOMMENDED	NICE TO HAVE

Develop a short-list of the Appendices you consider relevant to your business. Now is a good time to take a look at a list of potential Appendices for your business plan and select the ones you will use.

Actions

1. Go through the list of possible Appendices (see Steps 66 through 89, beginning on page 224). A Checklist download link is at the bottom of this page. Determine which Elements are relevant, and make a short-list of those you will add to your business plan as supporting information.

2. Create a place to store the information for each category as you collect it. For example, you might use a file box with different files for each category.

3. If you're using a computer and the Business Plan Shell™, go through the Appendices Section and delete each Appendix you will not use; then update the Table of Contents using the Table of Contents (ToC) function in your word processor.

4. As you gather the information for each Element of the Appendices, store it in the appropriate digital or hard-copy file.

Link: Download a free Appendices Worksheet from the page at **www.riskbuster.com/worksheet/12-appendices**

Tip: A business plan without adequate market research is like a house without a foundation.

Step 12: Brainstorm Products and Services

MUST HAVE	RECOMMENDED	NICE TO HAVE

You may have started your business idea with more than one product or service in mind. It can be healthy to brainstorm the topic of products and services to see what else might fit in your business idea.

Identify four to seven people you would like to participate, set a time for the brainstorming, contact them and explain what you want them to do and invite them to participate in the session. You will require a place where you can do the brainstorming without interruptions; your living room can work just fine if you unplug the telephones. Brainstorming is one of the most effective methods for gathering a lot of ideas quickly. It's amazing what can be achieved when you get several different minds focused on a problem or topic.

Brainstorming works best if all participants follow a few simple guidelines during the session. For example, ask that any critiquing or evaluation take place after the session, and offer these guidelines:

1. Brainstorm as many ideas as you can in the time allowed
2. All ideas are valid and recorded
3. Do not judge the ideas while brainstorming
4. Keep suggestions simple
5. Have fun!

Action

Gather a small group of people together to brainstorm your products and services. The actual session will probably take less than an hour, not counting time invested in organizing the session and the group.

Step 13: Prioritize Your Products and Services

MUST HAVE	RECOMMENDED	NICE TO HAVE

Focus your market research effort on the products and services most important to your business. You might wish to provide all the products and services in the world, but time, money, and energy require some prioritizing and focus. For most types of business, I recommend that you focus on twelve or fewer products, services, or lines. Select which ones you will focus on for your market research, and file the rest away for future reference.

From the list of products and services you brainstormed in Step 12 (see page 66), select those on which you will focus your research effort.

Define Your Units

Products and services move through the marketplace in units. Units are used in every Industry as a way of measuring and communicating about products and services. A unit can be a product, a service or a line of products or services. It can also be a package deal, consisting of either products or services or a combination of both. The table on the following page shows possible examples of units.

When arranging your products and services into units, keep two things in mind. First, know how your competitors sell their goods and services to customers and use the Industry standard for your type of business. Second, consider how the customer will buy the goods and services from your business. Vegetables are typically sold by the pound or by the bundle. Dinner is sold by the plate. Gravel is sold by the truckload in Canada and by the burlap sack in Honduras.

Link: Download a free Prioritizing Products and Services Worksheet from **www.riskbuster.com/worksheet/13-prioritizing-products-and-services**

DEFINING YOUR UNITS	
Unit	*Example*
A product	One of my units is a book (1 book = 1 unit).
An hour of service	Each hour your mechanic works on your car is one unit. For my business, each hour spent coaching entrepreneurs is a unit.
A day of service	A training business typically sells training by the day, sometimes by the half-day.
A package or bundle of products or services	The travel Industry often groups different combinations of hotel, airfare and food to form a package or bundle.
A product line	In retail businesses where prices, variety and the sheer number of products make it unrealistic to list every item, products are often grouped together, and a dollar value can become the unit for measuring purposes. For example, a gift store might consider all its candles as a line and use the average purchase by a customer as the unit value.

Tip: In determining units for your business, consider how the same products or services are sold by similar businesses and how they are purchased by customers. The building trades often communicate in terms of square feet of building or linear feet of material. For example, a roof might be bought or sold by the square foot, yard or meter.

Tip: When organizing your products and services into units, it makes sense to keep the number of units to twelve or fewer in order to make the forecasting manageable.

Prioritizing Products and Services

How do you prioritize your products and services? There are different views to consider.

PRIORITIZING YOUR PRODUCTS AND SERVICES	
Questions to Ask	*Things to Consider*
Does the product or service fit your business mission and goals?	Your business mission is to serve your customers. If your products or services do not fit your mission, you risk confusing your customers.
Will the product or service earn you money?	If the product or service doesn't earn you money, there has to be some other compelling reason to use it.
How much mark-up or profit will the product or service earn for your business?	It's not that *all* your products and services have to be high producers, but you definitely want high producers among your offerings.
How accessible is the product or service?	Limited accessibility can be a strength or a weakness. A product that is difficult to obtain can command higher prices and be a customer magnet.
How much control do suppliers exert over the product or service?	A supplier who has a monopoly will exert a lot of control over prices and terms.
How much control do the customers exert over the product or price?	Some suppliers will dictate consumer prices; others will give you more leeway. You will want to assess whether you need pricing flexibility in order to satisfy your customers.
Can you build or obtain the amount of product or service your customers will order?	If you are hoping to attract a large buyer, can you ramp up effectively to supply larger orders? Can you maintain profit levels while producing larger amounts?
Can you get the products or services to the customer in a timely, profitable manner?	I might like to sell books in far off countries, but is it realistic? It's unlikely that I can get books to someone in Asia in a timely manner until I have made distribution arrangements.

To keep things in perspective, depending on how well you already know your business, this might only be the first pass for your products and services. As you continue to research your market and become more knowledgeable about your business and Industry, you may find that you change your way of thinking many times between now and opening day. Stay curious, continue listening and keep an open mind. The only constant is change.

View this as an exercise to get you started on your market research–you have to begin somewhere. Start with the best list you can put together and let your customers guide you to fine tune it.

Prioritizing Products and Services Example

My concept began with a desire to serve entrepreneurs. I set out to establish a small business that markets a book, a CD and training resources for entrepreneurs. Here is a partial list.

PRODUCT OR SERVICE	UNITS
1. Books for Business Planners	Retail, Bookstore and Distributor Rates
2. Digital Tools for Business Planners	CD and Downloads from Website
3. Workshops for Business Planners	Day Rate, Half-Day Rate, Individual Seat

Actions

1. Review all your product and service ideas.

2. Prioritize which products and services you will focus on for market research purposes. If appropriate, keep the rest of the ideas for future reference.

3. Research businesses similar to yours; then arrange your products or services into units. Keep your short-list to twelve or fewer units if possible.

Step 14: Discover Your Assumptions

MUST HAVE	RECOMMENDED	NICE TO HAVE

It's difficult to recognize our assumptions, and it's nerve-wracking to change them. Most of us perceive our assumptions to be our reality. We believe things and therefore they are. In business, inaccurate assumptions can cost you your investment.

For a banker or a business analyst, few things are more frightening than an entrepreneur who has all the answers. We have all met such individuals. Because they already know everything, they tend to spend a lot more time talking than listening. Impassioned about their idea, they assault the marketplace. Armed with their bullet-proof rationales, they overpower anyone who might suggest a different view or method. The marketplace has a way of dealing with zealots who wear blinders; it's called bankruptcy, and it's always a disaster.

If you are serious about starting your business, classify everything not already proven as an assumption and then set out to prove or disprove everything you assume. This is much safer than making a few brash statements and then putting your equity on the line.

Link: Download a free Assumptions Worksheet from the page at **www.riskbuster.com/worksheet/14-assumptions**

Tip: As you research your market, be vigilant for assumptions that you missed in your first list. As you discover more assumptions, add them to your list. It may seem difficult to identify and adjust your own assumptions. Consider that any one of your assumptions, should they be wrong, could propel you into bankruptcy. Market research is a confidence builder!

Example: List of Assumptions

QUESTION	DAN'S ASSUMPTIONS
1. Who will buy your product or service?	Adult entrepreneurs, both male and female, who need to develop their own business plans.
2. What ages are your customers?	Hottest markets are 25 to 45 years old, male and female, and working adults from ages 20 to 55.
3. How many potential customers are there?	Perhaps 20 to 50% of people of workforce age.
4. Can you identify different groups or categories of customers?	Anyone thinking about getting into business, those already in the process of starting businesses, and business owners – located in Canada and the USA.
5. Why will customers buy your products or services?	To make the business planning process easier to navigate.
6. What are they currently buying to meet that need?	All nature of books and digital products that are only partially effective for novices.
7. How often will customers buy your product or service?	Once for themselves and perhaps more as gifts for family and friends.
8. Will customers come back and buy again?	There is potential to convince customers to purchase products as gifts for friends and family. Potential also exists to up-sell book buyers to purchase digital products and vice versa.
9. Will they send their friends to buy your products and services?	Will have to build-in incentives for this.

The preceding table is a partial list of the assumptions I actually listed and researched. The Worksheet on the next two pages will prompt you for a more complete list of your assumptions about your business idea.

Action

Using the following Worksheet or on a blank sheet of paper, write out a minimum of 20 assumptions. Don't stop until you have written down every wingding notion you ever had about your business idea. Write a hundred assumptions, if you have that many.

WORKSHEET: ASSUMPTIONS	
Question	*List of Assumptions*
1. Who will buy your product or service?	
2. What ages are your customers?	
3. How many potential customers are there?	
4. Can you identify different groups or categories of customers?	
5. Why will customers buy your products or services?	
6. What are they currently buying to meet that need?	
7. How often will customers buy your product or service?	
8. Will customers come back and buy again?	
9. Will they send their friends to buy your products and services?	
10. Will customers purchase your product or service as a gift for their family and friends?	

Question	List of Assumptions
11. What else do they buy?	
12. What magazines do they read?	
13. What TV programs do they watch?	
14. What hobbies do they enjoy?	
15. If your potential clients are businesses, how many are there?	
16. What type of businesses are your clients?	
17. How many people do they employ?	
18. What products and services do they sell?	
19. What size is your market area?	
20. Who are your competitors?	
21. How many competitors are there?	
22. Why do customers purchase from your competitors?	
23. Are customers pleased with the service they get from your competitors? If yes, why? If not, why not?	
24. Would your competitors' customers switch to your product or service; and what would it take to get them to do so?	

Step 15: Set Market Research Goals

MUST HAVE	RECOMMENDED	NICE TO HAVE

How do you research your market? You need to prove your business case. You must prove that your products and services will sell and make you a profit. Keep in mind that the time and energy invested in market research is for you. It is a confidence-building process that will enable you to decide whether or not to start your business. Each additional piece of research will either increase or decrease your confidence in your business idea. If you discover enough positives, you will start your business; negatives should cause you to back off or try different ideas until you get enough positives.

Secondary and Primary Market Research

When you set out to research your market, you will be exploring two main categories of research: secondary and primary. Secondary comes first, because you will do much of your secondary research before narrowing your focus to primary research. In other words, check out the big picture and then move into the smaller or more localized market research, beginning with a more general approach and moving to more specific.

Secondary market research is the information you will obtain from other sources, such as Statistics Canada or the US Bureau of the Census, reports, articles in trade or consumer magazines, and the Internet.

Primary market research is the information you gather yourself by talking with and surveying customers, competitors, and suppliers. Typical methods for conducting primary market research are observation, personal interviews, focus groups, formal surveys, mail surveys, and telephone surveys.

The following table offers a number of ideas on where to access information and assistance.

SOURCES OF ASSISTANCE AND INFORMATION	
□ Accountants	□ Family and Friends
□ Affiliations	□ Government Agencies
□ Associations	□ Individuals
□ Audio and Video Cassettes	□ Insurance Agents
□ Bankers	□ Internet
□ Books	□ Lawyers
□ Business Advisors	□ Libraries
□ Business Development Banks	□ Newspapers
□ Business Development Organizations	□ Census and Statistics Agencies
□ Chambers of Commerce	□ Publications
□ Conferences	□ State Government Agencies
□ Consultants	□ Tax Planners
□ Corporations	□ Competitors
□ Courses/Seminars/Workshops	□ Universities
□ Economic Development Officers	□ Yourself

Tip: The Internet has made it easier to research. It is unquestionably the largest collection of public information in the world, and it's growing every minute. Any of the sources in the table above can be located in moments by searching the Internet with your browser.

Dan's Strategic Market Research Objectives

After listing my assumptions and reviewing the Sources of Assistance and Information on the previous page, I wrote my list of strategic market research objectives. The following table includes some examples:

EXAMPLE: STRATEGIC MARKET RESEARCH OBJECTIVES		
Strategic Market Research Objectives	*Secondary*	*Primary*
1. Learn more about writing. I know some writers I can question.	Books, Associations	Workshops, Interviews
2. Learn more about entrepreneurs. Determine how many are out there, how many are in business, how many are starting businesses and how many are simply thinking about or wish to own a business.	Statcan, US Census, Government, Internet	Interviews, Surveys, Focus Groups
3. Learn more about business books and specifically any that compete with my book. I have a few in my library and I will begin gathering more.	Library, Books	Read books, use digital products
4. Learn more about every one of the assumptions listed in the previous step. I will have to obtain information from municipal, provincial and federal government and Industry sources in both Canada and the USA.	Read Trade Publications, Internet	Prove or disprove what I think I know

Actions

1. Write a list of your Strategic Market Research Objectives as you understand them at this moment. Don't worry about perfection or missed areas at this point. Write at least five to ten goals, more if you can.

2. Using the Sources of Information and Assistance checklist, identify potential secondary and primary sources for each of your strategic objectives.

3. Print or write your Strategic Market Research Objectives and hang copies in visible locations (your desk, your fridge, and your bathroom).

WORKSHEET: STRATEGIC MARKET RESEARCH OBJECTIVES		
Strategic Market Research Objectives	*Secondary*	*Primary*
1.		
2.		
3.		
4.		
5.		

Link: Download a free Strategic Market Research Objectives Worksheet at **www.riskbuster.com/worksheet/15-strategic-market-research-objectives**

Step 16: Write Market Research Questions

MUST HAVE	RECOMMENDED	NICE TO HAVE

The quality of your research will be partially determined by the quality of the questions you ask.

As a general strategy, you will want to glean all you can from secondary market research sources and then narrow your focus to primary. For now don't worry whether your questions can be answered through primary or secondary research. It's more important to clarify your questions, then to determine the best method to obtain the answers. If you're confused about this, re-read Step 10 (see page 60).

Example: List of Market Research Goals

Market Research Questions	Supporting Information	Where to Find Answers
1. How many people at any given time are attempting to start a business?	Existing Surveys, Research or Polls	Statcan, US Census, pollsters, Internet
2. Are there more men or more women starting businesses?	Existing Surveys, Magazine Articles	Provincial, State or National Studies, Internet
3. How many people are considering starting businesses?	University Studies or Papers	Universities, Internet
4. How many business owners will develop their own business plan?	Surveys, Testimonials	Probably have to survey business owners for this info
5. How many existing business owners would contract me to develop their business plan?	Surveys, Letters of Intent	Probably have to survey business owners for this info

Market Research Questions	*Supporting Information*	*Where to Find Answers*
6. How many entrepreneurs start their business without a plan?	Surveys	Probably have to survey business owners for this info
7. What meeting places do my customers have in common? Where can I get the most bang for my advertising bucks?	Magazine articles from credible sources	Search Inc, Entrepreneur and Profit magazine archives
8. How many of my customers own computers and have access to the Internet?	Statistics showing Internet usage growth	Internet, computer hardware and software magazines and businesses
9. Why do customers buy my competitors' products?	Interviews of competitors	Documentaries, videos, competitor advertisements
10. Why will customers pay for my book and digital products when there are free solutions?	Test marketing, selling samples to customers	Negotiate with existing customers

Link: Download a free Market Research Questions Worksheet at **www.riskbuster.com/worksheet/16-list-market-research-questions**

WORKSHEET: LIST OF MARKET RESEARCH QUESTIONS		
Market Research Questions	*Supporting Information*	*Where to Find It*
1.		
2.		
3.		

Actions

Write your market research questions.

1. Reread your List of Assumptions (see page 72) and your List of Market Research Objectives (see page 77).

2. Write a list of market research questions that you wish to have answers for. Try to have at least one question for each assumption and each objective.

3. Don't worry about missing questions at this point. If you are truly curious, many more questions will surface as you research. Later, as you think of other questions, add them to your list.

4. Go back and review the list of potential Sources of Assistance and Information. Consider where you can find answers to your questions. Make your list.

5. Use the preceding Worksheet as an example to create a table to list your questions, what you will seek in the way of supporting information, and where to find the answers you need.

Step 17: Prove Your Assumptions

MUST HAVE	RECOMMENDED	NICE TO HAVE

Become a super sleuth and set out to prove or disprove all of your assumptions. This is the work of researching your market. Armed with your List of Assumptions (see page 72), your List of Market Research Goals (see page 78), and your Market Research Questions (see page 81), it's time to venture out and learn.

The key to this step is to keep an open mind. Persist in digging up all available information.

Proving and Disproving Assumptions Example

I set out to prove or disprove my assumptions. One of the joys of market research is that it compels you to learn more about the world around you. I learned some interesting things along the way.

I get bogged down quickly at statistics sites; they tend to frustrate me and I'm not overly patient when searching. I want simple and understandable summary population tables, and I want them right now! On a number of occasions, I have emailed the contact links at the statistics websites requesting information. In most cases, I've received prompt and helpful responses to my queries.

It was after one such desperate plea that I was able to complete the following table. The important thing is not that my initial assumptions are accurate. My increased confidence arises from the fact that my assumptions and knowledge base are becoming more accurate.

Keep sifting until you have separated the wheat from the chaff to harvest the purest information for your efforts.

PROVING AND DISPROVING ASSUMPTIONS EXAMPLE		
Questions I Wish to Have Answered	*My Assumptions Before Researching*	*What I Know or Believe After Researching*
Population of my community	75,000	84,615
Percent of population considering business	7 percent of population–5,250	12 percent of labor force
Population of British Columbia	3,000,000	3,907,740
Total who could use my book in BC	210,000	201,854
Population of Canada	30,000,000	31,600,000
Total who might need my book in Canada	2,100,000	3,720,000
Population of United States	300,000,000	288,368,698
Total who might need my book in USA	21,000,000	34,604,244
Percentage of population who are entrepreneurs	10 percent	12 percent
Total potential book readers in Canada and USA	21,210,000	38,333,163
My Confidence in My Business Idea	**Less Confident**	**More Confident**

Actions

1. Research your market. Read trade journals and books, search on the Internet, review reports, ask questions, follow your hunches and turn over all the rocks.

2. Challenge your assumptions until they are either proven or disproven. Record your findings and adjust your thinking when necessary.

Step 18: List Key Points About Your Industry

| MUST HAVE | RECOMMENDED | NICE TO HAVE |

At this point you have gathered a lot of information about your Industry. It is time to bring that information together in preparation for writing a description of your Industry.

Ultimately this writing will end up in your business plan as the Industry Element (see page 127), but for now don't worry about the business plan, your reader, or getting it perfect. Simply write a list of important points you now know about your Industry.

North American Industry Classification System

The North American Industry Classification System (NAICS) is one of three main organizations in the world that deal with Industry classification. NAICS was developed by the statistical agencies of Canada, Mexico, and the United States. The organization of NAICS followed the North American Free Trade Agreement with a goal of creating common definitions and statistics to facilitate analysis of the three economies.

Here are a number of key points to help you understand your Industry:

- Industries are made up of businesses and other organizations that produce goods and services. All businesses produce either products or services or a combination of both.

- The agencies responsible for collecting taxes in each country are primary users and drivers of the Industry classification systems, because of their need to classify businesses for taxation purposes.

- NAICS analyses businesses according to their *business process* to determine what Industry they are in. Knowing this helped me to understand why certain types of businesses are grouped as they are, to make up some of the industries. As a writer I am grouped with artists and performers because my process for doing business is substantially the same as that of artists and performers.

The following table shows the 20 NAICS Industry sectors:

INDUSTRY SECTORS	
11 Agriculture, Forestry, Fishing, and Hunting	53 Real Estate, Rental and Leasing
21 Mining and Oil and Gas Extraction	54 Professional, Scientific and Technical Services
22 Utilities	55 Management of Companies and Enterprises
23 Construction	56 Administrative and Support, Waste Management and Remediation Services
31–33 Manufacturing	61 Educational Services
41 Wholesale Trade	62 Health Care and Social Assistance
44–45 Retail Trade	71 Arts, Entertainment and Recreation
48–49 Transportation and Warehousing	72 Accommodation and Food Services
51 Information and Cultural Industries	81 Other Services (except Public Administration)
52 Finance and Insurance	91 Public Administration

Link: Access the NAICS information at the US Census website at **www.census.gov/eos/www/naics**

Link: Access the NAICS information from Statistics Canada at **www.statcan.ca/english/concepts /Industry.htm#1**

Link: Download a free Key Industry Statements Worksheet at **www.riskbuster.com/worksheet/17-key-Industry-statements**

Example: Key Industry Statements

List of Key Points About Industry	Dan's List of Key Industry Statements
What Industry or industries is your business in?	• 71151 Independent Artists, Writers and Performers.
What quantities of goods are sold and what is the value of those goods?	• The 672 firms active in Canadian book publishing recorded revenues of more than $2.4 billion in the 2000–01 fiscal year, up 9.4 percent from the previous survey results in 1998–99 and a 20.0 percent increase from 1996–97. • John Kremer, in his book, *1,001 Ways to Market Your Books*, states: "More than 1,000 business titles are published every year [in the United States]. In 1996, business book publishers had $666 million in net sales."
What is the Industry outlook and growth potential?	• Business books are a hot market, and they tend to pick up sales momentum as time passes. Kremer states: • "Between 1991 and 1995, sales of business books [in the United States] increased by 26 percent. Books about small business are especially hot [Simba Information]." • "Business books, like children's books, sell better as time passes. Business books have a great backlist potential."
What are the Industry trends (past, present and future)?	• The book publishing Industry is growing. • E-books are the fastest growing area of the book publishing Industry. • In the micro-business arena, service type businesses are the fastest growing type of business.

List of Key Points About Industry	Dan's List of Key Industry Statements
What key points about your Industry help to support your business case?	<ul><li>In the United States, 10.1 million adults are engaged in trying to start new businesses at any given time.</li><li>Men are twice as likely to start a business as women.</li><li>Entrepreneurship involves adults at all ages, except those over 65 years.</li><li>The most active group are young men aged 25–34.</li></ul>
What population shifts and consumer trends affect your Industry?	<ul><li>Population figures for my target customer groups are generally increasing.</li></ul>
What are the main challenges faced by the Industry?	<ul><li>The Canadian book publishing Industry is challenged by a dependence on government grants and lower profitability, compared to foreign book publishers and agents.</li></ul>
What are the main barriers or incentives to entry by new businesses?	<ul><li>There are two main barriers to new independent writers entering the Industry: building of credibility and name recognition, and the high cost of marketing to penetrate the market.</li></ul>
What significant new developments have or are taking place in your Industry?	<ul><li>According to Kremer, "In 1970, there were about 3,000 independent small presses in the United States. In 1997, that number had grown to 60,000."</li></ul>

List of Key Points About Industry	Dan's List of Key Industry Statements
What is the size of the total market, and how is it divided up and served by your competitors?	• Business book sales have enjoyed a history of growth in Canada and the USA, and more growth is forecasted for the future. • According to the GEM 2002 study, about 286 million people, or *12 percent* of the 2.4 billion labor forces in the 37 GEM countries analyzed, are involved in new business formation.
What is the size of your local market?	• My primary market will be North America. • There were a total of 344,500 businesses in BC in 2001. Of these, 337,400 (98 percent) were small businesses. Over half (54 percent) of all businesses in the province were operated by a self-employed person without paid help. • The majority of small businesses in BC are micro businesses with less than five employees. In 2001, there were 279,800 small businesses of this description, representing 83 percent of all small enterprises. Over 55 percent of all small businesses were self-employed individuals without paid help. • Three-quarters of small businesses in BC are in the service sector.
What opportunities will your business take advantage of?	• To provide business planning solutions to those considering, starting, or growing a business.

Actions

To complete this task you must complete your secondary market research and then:

1. Determine which Industry or industries your business is in.

2. Research to find existing reports, articles, tables, or descriptions of your Industry or industries.

3. From your market research, identify and list the key points you wish to include in your Industry Element.

4. Using the table on the following page, review your list of key points to ensure that it is complete. Identify any missing information and add it to your list.

5. Organize your list of key points in preparation for writing your Industry Element.

Tip: After gathering and listing all the key information about your Industry, organize the information from general to specific. For example, you might consider, for your readers' sake, beginning with the larger picture (total Industry, national or international) and working your way to your more immediate situation, the local Industry picture. This will help you and your reader build a perspective on your Industry and how it relates to your business.

| WORKSHEET: KEY INDUSTRY STATEMENTS ||
List Of Key Points About Industry	*Your Key Industry Statements*
What Industry or industries is your business in?	
What quantities of goods are sold and what is the value of those goods?	
What is the Industry outlook and growth potential?	
What are the Industry trends (past, present and future)?	
What key points about your Industry help to support your business case?	
What population shifts and consumer trends affect your Industry?	
What are the main challenges faced by the Industry?	
What are the main barriers or incentives to entry by new businesses?	
What significant new developments have taken or are taking place in your Industry?	
What is the size of the total market, and how is it divided up and served by your competitors?	
What is the size of your local market?	
What opportunities will your business take advantage of?	

Step 19: Segment Your Market

MUST HAVE	RECOMMENDED	NICE TO HAVE

Identify different parts of your market to use as building blocks for researching your market, forecasting your sales, and developing your Marketing Action Plan.

Too often I encounter inexperienced entrepreneurs who say they plan to sell their product or service to a generic group called "all people." Aside from my gut instinct that this statement may never be completely accurate, it's not very useful for researching, planning, forecasting, or marketing purposes. It will be more effective to describe your market in more detail in order to arrive at a business and marketing plan that you can take to the bank. Dig deeper, narrow your focus, and strive to define your market and your customers as accurately as possible.

Here are five main categories of variables, different ways to segment or break your market into manageable groups:

- Geographic–where they live or work
- Demographic–age group
- Psychographic–needs or wants
- Behavioral–for example, "early adopters"
- Business–type of business, earnings, number of employees

Action

From your market research, write out a number of statements describing your customers.

Step 20: Write a Draft Description of Your Customers

MUST HAVE	RECOMMENDED	NICE TO HAVE

Bring together what you have learned about your target market and write a draft description of your customers.

When it comes to determining customer wants and needs, part of your market research may come from secondary sources, but ultimately you will need to survey real live customers in order to get the answers you need. At this point you have probably completed enough research to tackle the first draft of the Description of the Customers Element (see page 138).

Part of the objective with this step is to reveal what you still need to learn about your customers. Don't worry if you feel as though you don't have all of the answers at this point; if you have not yet done your primary market research, you may still have much to learn about your customers.

Actions

1. Using the statements you developed in Step 19 (see page 91) and all the information you've learned through your market research so far, write a draft description of your customers.

2. Identify what's missing from your description and clarify the questions you still need to answer and how to get those answers.

Link: Download a Statements Describing Customers Worksheet at **www. riskbuster.com/worksheet/18-statements-describing-customers**

Link: Download a free Draft Description of Customers Worksheet at **www.riskbuster.com/worksheet/19-draft-description-customers**

Step 21: Assess What You Are Learning

MUST HAVE	RECOMMENDED	NICE TO HAVE

Compare what you know now with what you previously thought to be true. This will provide you with a benchmark from which to identify missing information and next steps.

Example: Assessing What You Have Learned

Pre-Research Assumptions	What I've Learned So Far
1. My label for my customer will be an entrepreneur.	There are many different segments within this large group; self-employed, start-ups, incorporated, thinking about starting.
2. I think any entrepreneur over the age of 20 would read my book.	More clear now about common statistical groupings such as ages 20 to 54, my most probable readers.
3. After asking 200 people their opinion, I assumed that at least 7 percent of the population was at any given time considering starting a business.	I have shifted to 10% of those between the ages of 20 and 54; then further shifted to 12% of the total population. I'm not confident in either of these yardsticks yet; need to dig deeper.
4. The province I live in has about 3 million people in it.	According to the 2001 Census, it is actually 3,907,740 with 2,018,545 between the ages of 20 and 54.
5. Of 300,000,000, approximately 7 percent or 21,000,000 potential readers.	I now assume that my potential market is a minimum of 12 percent of 288,368,698, which is 34,604,244 people.

Actions

1. Reflect on what you've learned so far about your business.

2. Refer to Step 14 (see page 71) and re-read your original assumptions.

3. Review market research Steps 11 through 19 (see pages 65 to 91) and add any points that come up, such as new assumptions you have identified, questions that need to be answered, and key things you have learned.

4. List a minimum of ten things you have learned about your market and your business.

5. Make a list of any points that you still need to learn more about.

WORKSHEET: ASSESSING WHAT YOU HAVE LEARNED ABOUT YOUR BUSINESS	
Pre-Research Assumptions	*What I've Learned So Far*
1.	
2.	
3.	

Key Points You Still Need to Learn About

1. _____

2. _____

3. _____

Link: Download a free Assessing What You've Learned Worksheet at **www.riskbuster.com/worksheet/20-assessing-what-you-have-learned**

Step 22: Research Competitors

MUST HAVE	RECOMMENDED	NICE TO HAVE

Research and create a profile of your competitors. This may be one of the most daunting yet most revealing and rewarding steps in your market research.

Customers Buy for Their Reasons, Not Yours

Customers purchase products and services from competitors for their own reasons. You must understand those reasons in order to determine why customers will buy from you. Your competitors can be your greatest source of valuable information about the wants and needs of your customers. If you miss this step, you could be in for a rough ride.

Do not underestimate your competitors. They are in business because they understand their customers' wants and needs and they know how to sell their products and services to customers. No matter how many things your competitors might be doing wrong, they must be doing many things right to be in the market. You need to understand the good and the bad, the positive and the negative.

Direct and Indirect Competition

Your business will have direct and indirect competitors. A direct competitor sells the same products and services, competing for the same customers and sales. An indirect competitor sells entirely different products or services, and competes for the same funds from the customers' wallets. You will need to consider all the competitors in your scan and then determine the impact of each on your potential sales.

Who Are Your Competitors?

If you know who your competitors are, make a list of them. For some businesses, this can be as simple as going to the telephone directory; for others, the information can be more difficult to find.

How Will You Research Your Competitors?

Don't be timid when it comes to researching competitors. This is a task that must be taken seriously if you're going to succeed.

Here are some suggestions on how to research your competitors:

- Conduct a survey of your competitors.
- Research them on the Internet.
- Telephone them.
- Pose as a customer–call or visit and ask questions.
- Buy and analyze your competitors' product(s) or service(s).
- Join an association whose members are your competitors.
- Contact a competitor outside your market area, and ask if he or she will help you.
- Get a job and work for one or more of your competitors.
- Interview your competitors' customers.
- Read books, magazines, newspaper articles.
- Watch TV or other media coverage about your competitors.

Differentiation and Positioning

Differentiation is the term used to describe how you are different from your competitors.

Do you wish to be the cheapest, the fastest or the most convenient? Will you aspire to be the best in your arena and command the highest prices?

Tip: Positioning is a bit like a fine wine; it improves with age. Of course you want to nail it as closely as possible at the beginning of your business. Once you've defined your customer base reasonably accurately, test your assumptions by getting out there and making a few sales. Once you're in the marketplace, your customers will guide you in the fine tuning.

Example: Positioning Statements

The preceding study enabled me to begin to differentiate my business from the competitors' and to make the following positioning statements:

- Macrolink Action Plans Inc. will serve ordinary, down-to-earth entrepreneurs who will develop their own business plans. The service will not include developing business plans for customers.

- Books will be in the medium to high price range and in the high quality category.

- CD and digital downloads with be in the lower price and medium quality category.

- Books and digital products will be stand-alone, as well as integrated and offered in package deals.

- Customers will be male or female entrepreneurs, either considering, starting, or growing a small or micro business. The highest concentration will be in the service sector.

Actions

Here is one simple method for establishing how your business might be different from the others. Create an expanded version of the table like the following sample (with as many rows as you need, but at least seven). Determine what features or characteristics are most important to your customers. This information can be sourced from secondary sources, but it can also be determined from a market survey of your potential customers. It can also be learned through informal questioning and discussion with those who are knowledgeable about your products or services.

The table below can be used to differentiate your business or goods from the competition.

1. List your business in the first row.

2. List your top six competitors, more if you think it useful or necessary. Rank the competitors according to their importance to you, beginning with the most important.

3. List the features (price, quality, service) from left to right, according to their importance to the customer. Research to determine where each of the competitors is positioned with regard to each feature. For example, is the competitor's product high, low, or medium quality?

WORKSHEET: COMPETITIVE ANALYSIS					
COMPETITORS in order of their importance (or threat) to you	FEATURES in order of their importance to the customer				
	#1	#2	#3	#4	#5
1. Your Business					
2. Competitor #1					
3. Competitor #2					
4. Competitor #3					
5. Competitor #4					
6. Competitor #5					

Link: Download a free Competitive Analysis Worksheet at **www.riskbuster.com/worksheet/21-competitive-analysis**

Step 23: Prioritize and Target Customers

MUST HAVE	RECOMMENDED	NICE TO HAVE

At this point you should know your competitors quite well. You have learned how they serve their customers and gleaned what you can about what the customers need.

Now it's time to target your customers. Targeting your customer means deciding which market segment or segments to prioritize in order to focus your researching, selling, and marketing efforts.

Criteria for targeting:

- How attractive is the segment in terms of size and growth rate and potential sales?
- How many competitors are serving the segment?
- Is there a threat of substitutes?
- What is the bargaining power of the buyers and suppliers?
- Is the segment a fit for you in terms of your business resources, capabilities, skills and competitive advantage?

At this stage in my own research process, I found that I was using many different terms or labels to describe my potential customers. I recognized that I must somehow move away from the huge (albeit enticing) group described as "12% of the labor force in 40 countries," toward smaller, more definable, more reachable and manageable customer groups.

After some vigorous digging at the Statistics Canada and US Census websites, I developed the following table, which contains a more targeted definition of the customers for Macrolink Action Plans Inc.

Example: Description of the Customers

TOP PRIORITY	SECOND PRIORITY	THIRD PRIORITY
1 Million Workforce-Age People Starting Businesses in Canada, Male and Female	Economic and Enterprise Development Agencies in Canada and USA	18 Million Non-Employer Business Owners in Canada and USA
10 Million Workforce-Age People Starting Businesses in USA, Male and Female	Independent Distributors, Bookstores, Colleges and Libraries, Chains that Sell Books	Workforce-Age People Starting Businesses outside Canada and USA

Action

Identify and prioritize your most important target markets or customer groups.

TOP PRIORITY	SECOND PRIORITY	THIRD PRIORITY

Link: Download a free Target Market Priority Worksheet at **www. riskbuster.com/worksheet/22-target-market-priority**

Step 24: Clarify Primary Research Questions

MUST HAVE	RECOMMENDED	NICE TO HAVE

Now that you have a clearer idea of who you're targeting, it's time to clarify what you want to learn about your customers. What would you like to ask or confirm when speaking directly to potential customers? The following list of questions should get you started. Feel free to delete any that don't apply to your business or to add a few of your own.

Suggested Questions for Your Market Survey

1. Who are your customers? Approximately what age?
2. Are they male or female? What education?
3. Where do they live? Where do they work?
4. Do they purchase the goods you will provide?
5. How much money do they or would they spend on the products or services?
6. Where do they currently buy the products or services?
7. What do they like or dislike about the products or services they currently purchase?
8. Do they think their need for these products and services will be increasing or decreasing in the future?
9. Will they buy these goods in the next year? How often?
10. Will they buy this product or service from you? When?

Action

Write a list of questions to ask your customers.

Step 25: Gather Primary Research

MUST HAVE	RECOMMENDED	NICE TO HAVE

Primary market research is the information that you collect yourself, as opposed to data you might gather from other sources.

Many different methods exist for gathering primary market research, including talking to customers and surveying customers, competitors and suppliers. Typical methods for collecting primary market information include observation, personal interviews, focus groups, formal surveys, mail surveys, and telephone surveys.

Here are some points to consider in deciding which method or methods to use.

PRIMARY MARKET RESEARCH METHODS		
Method	*Pros*	*Cons*
Observation	• Inexpensive if you do it yourself • You are learning firsthand	• Time consuming • You may feel like you're spying
Personal Interviews	• Inexpensive if you do it yourself • An opportunity to develop relationships • Can lead to sales • People might share more	• Time consuming • You may feel awkward during the first few attempts • People may be less frank because they don't want to hurt your feelings
Personal Experience or Job	• Can view firsthand how things work • Earn while you learn	• Can take time • Ex-employers might be negative once you begin to compete

Method	Pros	Cons
Mail Surveys	▪ Inexpensive to distribute to target ▪ Can survey remotely ▪ Can reach targets not otherwise accessible	▪ Low return rate, mailed surveys are easy to throw in the garbage ▪ Many people are tired of being surveyed ▪ Might get less honest responses
Focus Groups	▪ Gather a lot of information ▪ Can benefit from the interaction between people with different perspectives	▪ Takes time to organize ▪ Can be more costly to conduct ▪ Requires skill to facilitate
Internet Surveys	▪ Inexpensive to conduct ▪ Limits your focus to those who use the Internet ▪ Can be very efficient to manage ▪ You can reach a very broad customer base	▪ Either need some Internet savvy or need to hire someone to set it up ▪ Once it is established, you still need to invite or attract people to participate ▪ You limit your survey to those with access to a computer and the Internet
Telephone Surveys	▪ Can reach a lot of people	▪ Takes skill and a thick skin to get through the negativity ▪ Many people are tired of intrusions on private time

Step 26: Create Your Survey Questionnaire

MUST HAVE	RECOMMENDED	NICE TO HAVE

Build a questionnaire that brings you the answers you haven't already gleaned from your secondary market research efforts.

Tips for Creating a Market Survey Questionnaire

Here are tips to help you stay on track with your market survey.

1. Keep the tone friendly.
2. Include an introduction at the beginning and a thank-you at the end.
3. Keep the overall form brief and easy to use.
4. Keep questions short, clear, and understandable.
5. Determine what you need to know first, then design the questions to get the right information.
6. Everyone is busy. Be sensitive to using other people's time.
7. Beware of asking for sensitive or private information.
8. Give choices so the customer can either circle or pick a number.
9. Allow space for the customer to write comments.
10. Make it optional for customers to include their name and contact information.
11. Keep it simple, but not too simple.
12. If appropriate, be sure to ask if they would purchase your product or service.
13. Consider offering a gift or prize to each person who completes your survey.

Example: Market Survey Questionnaire for Imported Giftware

1. Have you ever purchased or received as gifts any imported handmade giftware?
   Yes _____ No _____

2. Have you ever purchased or received as gifts handmade giftware from India or Pakistan?
   Yes _____ No _____

   If yes, what type of giftware?
   Wooden _____ Marble _____ Brass _____
   Copper _____ Cotton _____
   Other _____ Please specify: _____

3. Would you be interested in purchasing the above mentioned handmade giftware from India or Pakistan?
   Yes _____ No _____

   If yes, would the item be used:

   a. In your home for you or your family's enjoyment? _____
   b. As a gift? _____
   c. Other? _____ Please specify: _____

4. Do you know where to shop for such giftware?
   Yes _____ No _____

5. When buying foreign handmade giftware, what do you value the most? (On a scale of 1 to 4, list in order according to preference, where 1 is your most valued choice)
   Craftsmanship _____ Cost _____ Uniqueness _____

   Other _____ Please specify: _____

Market Survey FAQs

1. **What am I trying to achieve by surveying my customers?** You are trying to learn more about your customer and your business. You can pick up general knowledge from secondary sources, but it is really your primary research–communicating directly with customers–that brings the specific knowledge about your customers in your market area. Ultimately, you are attempting to prove or disprove your own assumptions about your customers, your products and services, and your market.

2. **How many surveys should I do?** This will be different for each situation. A business that has only a few potential customers does not require the same number of surveys as a business with a potential market of thousands. I recommend getting a few questionnaires out, perhaps 10 or 20, followed by a revision of your survey as feedback dictates. Once you are confident that you are getting the information you need, you can then have another 50 people complete the survey. Assess the information you are getting, and do this again. I suggest doing 50 at a time until you find that your results level off or the information appears to provide you with a consistent message. One hundred samples generally bring a 10% chance of error, while 500 can give a 5% chance of error.

3. **When does my surveying stop?** In one way or another, you will always be surveying as long as you're in business. For your start-up survey, the time to stop is when you have enough answers to prove or disprove your assumptions and you cease to learn new information from the surveys. Your surveying just changes focus as your business evolves. As you do your surveys, your confidence level in your business idea will either increase or decrease.

4. **How do I ensure that people will complete my surveys?** If you are providing needed products or services and targeting the right customers, your job should be easier because they will be interested in what you're offering. Part of the answer is to take the time to define or target your customers. Once you are sure you're surveying the right people, choose a method that

fits the group you're targeting. For example, if they are really busy, make sure your survey is quick and easy to complete. If they use the Internet, perhaps a Web-based survey is the answer. Finally, you can offer incentives, such as entering each completed survey into a prize draw.

5. **When should I survey?** You certainly must survey potential customers prior to starting your business. Your customer service surveys will go on for the life of your business. You should survey for each new product, service, division, or business. You can survey to determine pricing, client preferences, changes in the marketplace, and competitor characteristics.

Actions

1. Review the sample questionnaire in this Step.

2. Select which method or combination of methods you will employ to gather your primary research.

3. Develop a list of questions to include in your survey questionnaire.

Tip: Don't underestimate yourself as an important source of market research. If you are getting into a business you know a great deal about, you are probably one of the best sources of market research. Your time working in the Industry counts—be sure to use it!

Step 27: Survey Your Customers

MUST HAVE	RECOMMENDED	NICE TO HAVE

It's important to learn firsthand knowledge about your customers. This is the step most newcomers fear and avoid. Get out there and mingle.

Actions

1. Review your business start-up goal in Step 5 (see page 55).

2. Determine when you must complete your surveying in order to meet your overall business planning goals.

3. Identify those you wish to survey.

4. Plan your approach. Will you telephone, speak in person, mail, or email?

5. Contact the customers and determine whether they will participate.

6. Be clear about your expectations and timelines. If possible, arrange in advance a time and place to pick up the completed survey form.

7. If you plan to follow up with a personal interview, make those arrangements.

8. Deliver the survey form to the customer; hand deliver if practical and possible.

9. Pick up the completed form at the agreed time and place.

10. Meet with the customer to complete the personal interview.

11. Follow up with a thank you card, message, or gift.

Step 28: Compile Survey Information

MUST HAVE	RECOMMENDED	NICE TO HAVE

This is a step that you may repeat, depending how much surveying or how many different surveys you do. Consider compiling the data in a spreadsheet. You will want to look for trends, patterns, and commonalities. If your survey questionnaire is well designed, this step should be relatively simple.

Action

1. Create an electronic or hard copy form in which to record the information you've collected through your surveys.

2. Review the information to determine what the surveys are telling you, or teaching you, about your business.

3. Using key points learned from your surveys, write a few clarifying statements about your customers.

Link: You will find links to a few web-based survey options at the Market Research SpringBoard at **www.riskbuster.com/ member/market-research-springboard**

Tip: If you are not getting clear answers or direction from your surveys, consider changing your questions. Remember, the quality of your questions determine the value of the answers.

Step 29: Revise Description of Customers

MUST HAVE	RECOMMENDED	NICE TO HAVE

Revisit the draft description of your customers written in Step 19 (see page 91). Consider whether the profile of your customer has changed because of what you've learned from surveying your market.

What you're striving for is to describe at least your primary and secondary customers. Don't get too bogged down with detail. At the same time, don't make it so light that you can't have confidence in the sales forecast. Your confidence level is one way for you to measure how realistic your figures are. If your forecast makes you nervous, imagine what it would do for a banker!

Yes, this can be difficult. If it were easy, everyone would own a business and more business owners would have written business plans.

Action

Beginning with the description of your customers, and using relevant information learned to date, rewrite the description of your customers. Do this only if you feel it necessary. Your first draft might be just fine.

Tip: Every ounce of time invested in revisions will save those reading your business plan a pound of time and potential frustration as they try to understand your business. If you're applying for a loan, this can be the difference between a positive or negative outcome or response to your application.

Step 30: Make a Go/No-Go Decision

MUST HAVE	RECOMMENDED	NICE TO HAVE

Decide whether or not to complete your business plan.

There will come a time to assess whether you have reached your main market research destination, to have enough information to be able to make a go or no-go decision. This is also referred to as proving your business case (see Step 10 on page 60).

Use the table on the following page to list and assess how comfortable you are with the proof you have gathered so far. Make note of any areas that need further market research or strengthening, and complete those tasks. Work with this step until you have enough information to decide whether to complete your business plan.

Choosing the Right Business Opportunity

Aside from financial considerations, numerous other factors could affect your decision.

- Will the business meet your financial goals?
- Will the business bring you the lifestyle you desire?
- Do you enjoy the work you will be doing?
- Has it been a lifelong dream that will preoccupy you until you pursue it?
- Will it enable you to locate and live in a desirable area?
- Are there more attractive opportunities for your investment?
- Can you afford to lose your investment if the business doesn't succeed?

Link: Download a free Proving Your Business Case Worksheet at ***www.riskbuster.com/worksheet/24-proving-your-business-case***

Actions

1. Use the following Proving Your Business Case Worksheet to create your own version, and list the ways you have proven your business case.

2. Using the following Feasibility and ROI Worksheet, determine if your business idea is viable or feasible, and calculate the return on your investment.

3. Compare the return on your investment with other investment opportunities.

4. Decide whether to complete a business plan for this venture.

WORKSHEET: PROVING YOUR BUSINESS CASE	
Have You Proven...?	*How?*
1. Your customers are real and that there is a strong demand for your products and services?	
2. The size of your market?	
3. You're qualified to run your business?	
4. You can supply your products and services?	
5. Your pricing is acceptable to your customers?	
6. Your business is financially viable?	
7. Your business is sustainable?	
8. You can mitigate risks and meet all of the applicable regulatory requirements?	
9. Have you proven your business case?	

Feasibility and Return on Investment (ROI)

The following table provides you a process to determine whether your business is viable. It also guides you to consider the return you will earn on your investment. By the time you reach this step, you should have gathered the necessary information to complete this task. Any missing information points to a need for more market research.

WORKSHEET: FEASIBILITY AND RETURN ON INVESTMENT	
Feasibility Step	*Results*
1. Determine Total Market Potential	
2. Calculate Market Share (Sales)	
3. List Cost of Building, Fixtures, Equipment	
4. Estimate Cost of Merchandise	
5. Calculate Operating Expenses	
6. Budget for Other Expenses	
7. Subtract Expenses from Sales	
8. Calculate Return on Investment	
9. Make Your Go/No-Go Decision to Complete a Business Plan	

Link: Download a free Feasibility and Return on Investment Worksheet
www.riskbuster.com/worksheet/25-feasibility-and-return-investment

Calculating Return on Investment

To calculate your return on investment (ROI), divide your profit after taxes by your total investment (times 100), as follows:

Profit After Taxes ÷ Total Investment x 100 = ROI

The following Worksheet will help you compare your return with potential returns on other investments:

WORKSHEET: RETURN ON INVESTMENT COMPARISION			
Profit	*Invest-ment*	*x 100*	*ROI*
Your Business $	$	x 100	%
Bank Account $	$	x 100	%
Tax Shelter $	$	x 100	%
$	$	x 100	%
$	$	x 100	%
$	$	x 100	%

Encouragement for the Weary Business Planner

If you have arrived at this point and determined that your business is not feasible, you might have just saved yourself a lot of heartache. If you have determined that your business is feasible and feel confident it can succeed, you have probably completed the most difficult part of the business planning process, your market research. The next steps should go quite quickly. You're a lot closer to completion than you might think!

Link: Download a free Return on Investment Comparison Worksheet at **www.riskbuster.com/worksheet/26-return-investment-comparison**

Build Your Business Concept Section

In order to create an introduction to you and your business, in this Section you will clarify who you are, where your business is positioned, and what you are selling.

Here are the five Elements in this Section and the corresponding RoadMap™ steps:

BUSINESS PLAN ELEMENT	ROADMAP STEPS
The Business	31
Products and Services	32
The Industry	33
The Owner	34
Strategic Goals and Objectives	35

If you have not already done so, I recommend that you begin to do your writing directly into a draft copy of your business plan.

Read the Business Concept Section of the Macrolink Business Plan to get a sense of what you are trying to achieve in this Section.

Link: Download the Business Plan Shell™ from the website at **www.riskbuster.com/member/member-resources**

Link: Download the Macrolink Business Plan from the website at **www.riskbuster.com/content/business-plan**

Step 31: Describe Your Business

MUST HAVE	RECOMMENDED	NICE TO HAVE

The Business Element is a snapshot of your present situation; the current condition of your organization.

This activity requires that you have completed a substantial amount of your market research, and that you understand your business well enough to write a description of your concept.

Three Vital Business Planning Benefits

Three highly beneficial things will occur when you write your business plan.

1. The writing will begin to shape the business. After scrawling out the rough draft and then referring to it later to make revisions, you will find you can identify weaknesses and pick out the holes in your description and in your thought process.

2. The process of writing will help you to identify and set goals. Incomplete tasks or missing information may indicate a need to research further.

3. You will find that you are able to communicate your business idea more clearly to others.

Link: Download a free Business Plan Elements Checklist from **www.riskbuster.com/worksheet/65-business-plan-elements-checklist**

Tip: Keep your reader in mind when writing the Elements of your business plan. What do you want your reader to know about your business?

The Business Element has the following five segments:

1. Identity Statement
2. Mission Statement
3. Vision Statement
4. Description of the Business
5. Legal and Regulatory

1. Identity Statement

Your identity statement should be simple and factual, and it must communicate the answers to the following questions:

1. What is the name of your company?
2. What is the legal form or structure of your business?
3. Where is the business headquartered, licensed, and registered?
4. When did or when will your business start?
5. What is the nature of your business (home-based, retail, services, or products)?
6. What is the scope of your business (local, regional, national, international, or global)?
7. What Industry is your business in?

Action. Using the questions and example below as a guide, write your identity statement (70 words or less) and enter it into the working copy of your business plan.

Example: Identity Statement

Macrolink Action Plans Inc is a privately held corporation headquartered in Prince George and registered in the Province of British Columbia. Founded in 1987, the business has focused mainly on delivery of training throughout Northern BC. This business plan is the owner's roadmap to reconfigure the business and implement a new marketing strategy for growth. The owner and principal shareholder is Dan Boudreau.

2. Mission Statement

Your mission statement should be clear and factual and it must communicate the answers to these questions:

1. What business are you in?
2. What product(s) or service(s) do you provide?
3. Who are your customers?
4. What is your competitive advantage?

Example: Mission Statement

> Macrolink provides practical and affordable business planning solutions for ordinary people with extraordinary business ideas.

Action. Using the questions and example above as a guide, write your mission statement (20 words or less) and enter it into the working copy of your business plan.

3. Vision Statement

Your vision statement should be succinct and it must communicate the answers these questions:

1. What kind of company do you want to be?
2. How do you wish to be viewed by the individuals and communities you serve?
3. How will you treat your customers, both internal and external?

Example: Vision Statement

> Macrolink Action Plans Inc. is the resource of choice for entrepreneurs, ensuring customer satisfaction every time.

Action. Using the preceding questions and example as a guide, write your vision statement (20 words or less) and enter it into the working copy of your business plan.

4. Description of the Business

Your description of the business should communicate the answers to these main points and questions:

1. Briefly describe your customers.

2. Describe your office.

3. Describe any other facilities (plant, warehouse, storefront, or field operations).

4. Describe your method of operation. Do you create products or purchase them from suppliers? Do you go to your customers, or do they come to you?

5. What equipment do you own or have to buy?

6. What are the outstanding characteristics (price, quality, selection, etc.) of your business?

Example: Description of the Business

Customers are entrepreneurs, business counsellors, and trainers. This includes clients from many areas of the globe, encompassing all range of start-ups, new firms, economic development organizations and business financing agencies. The primary market will be entrepreneurs from Canada and the USA.

Macrolink is a home-based business, with the majority of client interactions taking place either at the customer's location, by telephone or via email and the Internet.

Action. Using the key points and preceding example as a guide, develop a description of your business and enter it into the working copy of your business plan.

5. Legal and Regulatory

Keeping your reader in mind, this topic should cover any important legal and regulatory considerations. Answer the following questions:

1. Have you checked the zoning for your location to ensure that it is appropriate for your business?

2. Have you researched the taxation requirements and taken the necessary action?

3. Have you researched the Workers' Compensation Board requirements and taken the necessary action?

4. Which other regulatory agencies will affect your business, and what action have you taken for each?

5. Write out your contact information; this includes your street address, mailing address, Internet address, email address, telephone number, cell phone number, fax number, etc. If you're using a computer, this information should go into your header or footer.

Example: Legal and Regulatory

Macrolink's main mailing address is Box 101, Prince George, BC V2L 4R9. The main phone number is 1-250-612-9161. The company hosts a website at www.riskbuster.com. Boudreau can be reached via email at danb@riskbuster.com.

Action. Using the preceding questions and example as a guide, write your legal and regulatory segment and enter it into the working copy of your business plan.

Putting Your Business Concept Together

Your Business Element consists of the five segments you've now completed: Identity Statement, Mission Statement, Vision Statement, Description of the Business, and Legal and Regulatory. If you have completed each of the segments separately and now have five separate parts of The Business Element, it's now time to bring them all together to create a cohesive snapshot of your business.

Action. Your next task is to write a draft copy of your Business Element, using the following process:

1. Get a blank sheet of paper or a clean page in the digital working copy of your business plan.
2. Write the name of your business at the top of the page.
3. Ink or copy in your Identity Statement.
4. Insert your Mission Statement.
5. Enter your Vision Statement.
6. Write or copy in your Description of the Business.
7. Enter your Legal and Regulatory segment.
8. Read it aloud to yourself or have someone read it to you.
9. Revise until it accurately communicates your message.

Summary

One of the greatest benefits of creating a business plan is that you can use the information in various ways to operate your business. The information in this Element can be useful for:

- Creating marketing materials (business cards and brochures).
- Assembling sales letters and other communication tools.
- Copying to other Elements of your business plan to serve as starting points.
- Repurposing to become part of the Executive Summary.
- Communicating with employees.
- Developing proposals.

Tip: Although this Element covers a lot of key points about your business, keep it brief. When finished, it might be a short as a couple of paragraphs and in some cases as long as two pages. You will be going into much more detail about each topic in other Elements of your business plan.

Step 32: List Your Products and Services

MUST HAVE	RECOMMENDED	NICE TO HAVE

Describe the products and services your business will sell.

Example: Products and Services

Product or Service	*Units*
1. Books for Business Planners	Retail, Bookstore, and Distributor Rates
2. Digital Tools for Business Planners	CD and Downloadable from Website
3. Workshops for Business Planners	Day Rate, Half-Day Rate, Individual Seat
4. Facilitator Manuals for Counselors and Trainers	Retail Rate
5. Consulting and Business Plan Coaching	Hourly and Daily Rates

Assess Your Product or Service

Here are a number of questions to help assess a product and service:

1. **Is it simple?**
   Complexity repels customers. Even if something is complex, it must be presented to the customer in a simple form.

2. **Is it a building block?**
   Larger complex projects or products should be broken down into smaller building blocks.

3. **Is it scalable?**

   Can the project or product be mass-produced or delivered to large numbers of clients efficiently?

4. **Is it profitable?**

   Is the product or service profitable at lower and higher levels of production?

5. **Can it be sold effectively through the Internet?**

   Is the product digital or can distribution channels be arranged to efficiently provide to customers?

6. **Is it free from glue?**

   Is the product or service mired in government regulations, politics, or bureaucratic processes?

7. **Is it a one-person purchase?**

   Whenever a buying decision must go through one or more committees, the sales process is more cumbersome and therefore more expensive.

8. **Is it within your timelines?**

   Can you produce and provide the product or service to customers at critical times?

9. **Is it controllable?**

   There are many threats to project or product control. Understanding these threats entails Industry savvy and market research. Examples of threats are existing or new government regulations, supplier power or changes, natural disasters, and Industry trends.

10. **Can you afford it?**

    This information can be obtained only through a detailed financial plan.

Link: Download a free Products and Services Worksheet from **www.riskbuster.com/worksheet/27-products-and-services**

Tip: The more widespread a problem is, the larger the potential market or number of customers for the solution.

Selling the Benefits

As a business owner, one of the greatest skills you can cultivate is to be able to understand how your customer thinks in order to see what he or she needs and wants. This skill will enable you to identify the benefits to your customers.

Sell the benefits, or to use a popular phrase, "Sell the sizzle, not the steak." This works for a number of different business and personal situations, the most obvious being the selling of your products or services. Selling the benefits also works for negotiating, be it for writing employee contracts, serving customers, writing proposals, creating business plans, making arrangements with family, or mapping out your own life goals.

It is important to understand the difference between features and benefits. Features are about the product or service, whereas benefits are about what the product or service will do for the customer.

Turning Problems into Features and Benefits

Businesses solve problems for customers. The nature of the problem determines the features and therefore the benefits, to customers. For example, most of my work involves my computer. I travel a lot and need ready access to my computer files. I also need to be able to work while away from my office. The problem was that my old PC was not easily transportable. Other people had this problem as well. Along came the laptop computer, solving the problem for me and many other customers. My laptop computer is lightweight and easy to carry wherever I go, making it possible for me to have my office and personal information with me wherever I am. The features are translated to benefits.

How do you turn features into benefits? The key is to listen to your customers first, to ensure that you are solving real problems and meeting real needs. Once you clearly understand your customer's needs, you can then design the features and communicate the benefits.

The manufacturer or service provider defines and creates features to serve what the customers want as benefits. The manufacturer did its homework before, during, and after making my laptop.

Here is what you are faced with at the beginning of the business process. You need to somehow get into the customer's head and determine what the benefits are so you can ensure that your product or service meets the customer needs. How? Simply talk to your prospective customers. Describe what you wish to create for them; describe your product according to features. Ask your customers what they need and listen to their answers.

What's the Fuss About Competitive Advantage?

Your competitive advantage is something that sets you apart from the competition and hopefully compels customers to buy from you. Here are some examples:

A Unique Product	The Cheapest	The Fastest
Most Convenient	Superior Technology	Secret Formula

The following table shows the Macrolink products and services, features, benefits, and the competitive advantage for each.

Example: Competitive Advantage

Service or Product	*Features*	*Benefits*	*Competitive Advantage*
Coaching Service	♦ Affordable ♦ Effective ♦ Efficient	♦ Save money ♦ Get results ♦ Save time	A seasoned entrepreneur in your corner

Actions

1. Use the Products and Services Worksheet (below Task 4 in this list) or another suitable method and list your products and services.

2. Using the Competitive Advantage Worksheet (below Task 4 in this list), develop a list of the main features, benefits and competitive advantage for each product and for each service.

3. Copy your list of products and services directly into the Products and Services Element of your business plan.

4. If you think it appropriate, copy the list of features and benefits into your business plan.

WORKSHEET: PRODUCTS AND SERVICES	
Product or Service	*Units*
1.	
2.	
3.	

WORKSHEET: COMPETITIVE ADVANTAGE			
Product or Service	*Features*	*Benefits*	*Competitive Advantage*
1.			
2.			
3.			

Link: Download a free Competitive Analysis Worksheet from **www.riskbuster.com/worksheet/28-competitive-advantage**

Step 33: Describe Your Industry

MUST HAVE	RECOMMENDED	NICE TO HAVE

This Element of your business plan is a snapshot of the Industry or industries in which your business will compete.

Example: Description of the Industry

Macrolink sells its products and services to entrepreneurs in virtually all sectors and industries, primarily in Canada and the United States. For taxation purposes, the business is classified in the Independent Artists, Writers and Performers Industry. From a practical standpoint, the business provides its products and services to anyone considering, starting, or growing a business.

The Macrolink business case is built on providing practical and affordable business planning solutions to entrepreneurs who need to develop their own business plans. The owner estimates the potential market in Canada and the United States to be more than $110,000,000.

The outlook for the sale of business books is strong and positive. According to Industry authorities, business books are a hot market and tend to pick up sales momentum as time passes. Books about small business are especially hot and have excellent backlist potential.

The Macrolink business case is based on the following Industry trends and factors:

1. It is generally getting more complex to start and to operate a business, making it more important than ever for entrepreneurs to develop business plans.

2. How-to e-books are the fastest growing area of the book publishing Industry.

3. In the United States, 10 million adults are engaged in trying to start new businesses at any given time.

4. In British Columbia in 2004, 98 percent were small businesses; 83 percent were micro businesses with fewer than 5 employees; and 54 percent were single owners with no paid help.

5. Entrepreneurship involves adults of all ages, with the exception of people over 65 years old.

6. Young men aged 25–34 are the most active group involved in starting businesses, followed by women in the same age group.

7. Globally, the market for business planning products is huge. The GEM 2003 study showed that more than 300 million people of the 2.4 billion labor force in the 40 countries analyzed, are nascent entrepreneurs involved in new business formation.

The main barriers to selling business planning products and services are standing out from the many similar products and services, gaining brand recognition, and getting distribution.

The Opportunity

For most people considering starting a business, the realization that they need a business plan is like hitting a wall. This generates a great deal of frustration and causes many potential business owners to either give up on their business idea or push ahead into business without a business plan. The current situation allows room in the market for *practical and affordable products* that make the task of business planning manageable for entrepreneurs who realize they need to build their own business plans.

Action

To complete this Element you must first do your secondary market research and then develop your list of key information in Step 18 (see page 84). By now you will also have completed some or all of your primary market research and added useful local information to your library of information about your business. Using all the information gathered, write a description of your Industry or industries, including the following points:

1. Tell which Industry or industries your business is in.

2. Describe the quantity and value of goods sold.

3. Describe the Industry outlook and growth potential.

4. List the past, present, and future Industry trends.

5. Explain any key points about your Industry that help support your business case.

6. Chart or describe relevant population shifts and consumer trends.

7. Describe the main challenges faced by the Industry.

8. Describe any barriers or incentives to entry by new businesses.

9. Describe any new developments in the Industry.

10. Describe the size of the total market and your local market area.

11. Describe the opportunity or gap your business will serve.

Tip: Nobody expects you to become an economist in order to start your small or micro business. Your most important goal with this Element is to clarify that you understand the Industry your business is in. Keep this Element simple and practical.

Step 34: Write Your Biography

MUST HAVE	RECOMMENDED	NICE TO HAVE

Provide a brief introduction of you, the owner(s) of the business.

Many people find it difficult to write about themselves. This is an opportunity to tell about your strengths. In this Element you must communicate about your achievements in a positive way, without bragging.

Example: The Owner

Dan Boudreau is the sole owner, President and CEO for the business:

- Involved in small business development since 1980 as owner, coach, trainer, and consultant.
- Worked in community economic development for 15 years.
- Served 10 years on Finance and Lending Committee for a $5 million loan fund for entrepreneurs.
- Manages a $15 million fund that provides grants for economic development projects.
- Nominated twice as Entrepreneur of the Year–1997 and 1999.
- Develops and delivers workshops for entrepreneurs (Business Planning, Train the Trainer).
- Published Dream Catcher Business Planning Toolkit and Scratchpad (since 1995).

Boudreau's resumé is in Appendix A and a list of references is in Appendix B.

Actions

To complete this Element you will need to gather information about yourself that is relevant to the business you are starting, then:

1. Provide a brief snapshot of yourself, including any relevant educational or business achievements.

2. Briefly outline your work experience and training as it relates to the specific business you plan to start.

3. List your strengths and what you feel you will contribute to the business to make it successful.

4. List your relevant achievements and successes.

5. Note that your detailed resumé in the Appendices will support this Element.

Tip: If you haven't already done so, set up a working copy of the Business Plan Shell™ to do your writing. The Shell™ is on the RiskBuster™ CD or it can be downloaded free from the RiskBuster™ site at **www.riskbuster.com/member/member-resources**.

Step 35: Develop Your Strategic Plan and Goals

MUST HAVE	RECOMMENDED	NICE TO HAVE

Build your strategic plan and short-term business goals.

Example: Strategic Plan and Goals

Macrolink strategies include:

1. Effective financial management.
2. Effective marketing strategy for positive organizational growth.
3. Continuous research, development and innovation.
4. Advancement of service and product quality.
5. Effective communication with all stakeholders.

The short-term business goals are:

GOALS	TIMELINES
1. To publish printed books and e-books.	July 2009
2. To create a website with shopping cart.	August 2009
3. To launch the website, book, and ebooks.	September 2009
4. To achieve gross revenues of $128,242 for Year One.	September 2010
5. To retain net income before taxes of $12,061 for Year One.	September 2010

Link: Download a free Strategic Plan Worksheet from **www. riskbuster.com/worksheet/29-strategic-plan**

Actions

To complete this Element you will need to have completed most of your primary and secondary market research and then do the following:

1. Using your Mission and Vision Statements as a base, develop three to six strategic objectives for your business. Strategic objectives are broad in scope and more general, less specific than goals.

2. Set goals for Year One. Some areas to consider setting short-term goals are gross revenues, net profits, the number of units to be sold, the number of employees, new products and services, diversification, quality, customers, growth, return on investment, and training and professional development. Set goals only for the ones that are most important to you.

3. Prioritize your goals and determine who will perform each.

4. Set deadlines for completion (if applicable).

5. Copy the appropriate information from this segment into the Strategic Plan and Goals Element of the business plan.

WORKSHEET: STRATEGIC PLAN
Objectives
1.

WORKSHEET: GOALS AND TIMELINES	
Goals	*Timelines*
1.	
2.	

Link: Download a free Goals and Timelines Worksheet at **www.riskbuster.com/worksheet/30-goal-and-timelines**

Map Your Marketing Section

The purpose of this Section is to plan and describe how you will get your goods into the hands of paying customers.

Here are the ten business plan Elements in this Section and the corresponding RoadMap™ steps:

BUSINESS PLAN ELEMENT	ROADMAP STEPS
Market Area	36
Location: Marketing	37
Profile of the Customers	38
Competition and Differentiation	39
Sales and Distribution	40
Servicing and Guarantees	41
Image	42
Advertising and Promotion	43
Pricing Strategy	44
Marketing Action Plan	45

Read the Marketing Section of the Macrolink Business Plan to get a sense of what you are trying to achieve in this Section.

Link: Download a copy of the Macrolink Business Plan from **www.riskbuster.com/content/business-plan**

Step 36: Describe Your Market Area

MUST HAVE	RECOMMENDED	NICE TO HAVE

Define the geographic area in which your business will operate.

Market area can be defined a number of different ways. It can be a geographical area, a definite area that can be marked on a map. It might also be a building, a neighborhood, a city, a reserve, a region, a tribal council jurisdiction, a province, a country, or the entire globe.

Example: Market Area

> Macrolink will offer its hard-copy business planning solutions to clients throughout North America, and its digital products to anyone who can access the Internet.

Action

To complete this Element you will need to have completed most of your primary and secondary market research, and then write a description of the geographic area in which your business will operate.

Link: Download a free Market Area Worksheet from the website at **www.riskbuster.com/worksheet/31-describing-your-market-area**

Tip: This Element can be text, but a small map or picture might make it more effective.

Step 37: Describe Your Location

MUST HAVE	RECOMMENDED	NICE TO HAVE

Determine where to locate your business in terms of customers, marketing, and sales. This Element requires that you think about the issues of communicating and getting your products or services to your customers. Further, it pushes you to make some fundamental decisions. Questions to consider:

- Will your business be home-based or storefront?
- Does the business require walk-in traffic?
- Should you locate near your supply or raw materials?
- If you're shipping goods, do you need to be located near rail, road, water, or air transportation arteries?
- Do you need electrical, telephone, or Internet access?
- Where and how are similar businesses set up?

Example: Location Marketing

From a marketing perspective, Macrolink is located in the city of Prince George in North Central British Columbia. The city has the necessary infrastructure to enable Macrolink to operate globally through the use of its technology. The highway and air transportation infrastructures support travel to and from most of the major cities, making it easy to ship products and attend events.

Actions

To complete this Element you will need to:

1. Determine the best location for your business in relation to your customers.

2. Decide whether the business will be home-based, commercial, retail, urban, or rural.

Step 38: Describe Your Customers

MUST HAVE	RECOMMENDED	NICE TO HAVE

Develop a market profile using primary and secondary sources to identify the key information.

You will have written a draft description of your customers in Step 20 (see page 92) and then fine-tuned it in Step 29 (see page 110).

Example: Profile of Customers

Macrolink's primary customers will be entrepreneurs in Canada and the United States. In the 25 to 54 age group, Canada hosts 13,440,355 and the United States 122,718,203, totalling more than 136 million people in the ideal business planning age group. If only 12% of this group were involved in entrepreneurial activity, this would be a potential market of more than 16 million. In a 1999 Yankelovich poll, over one-third of Americans predicted they would own their own business within a decade.

Characteristics of this client group are shortage of time, scarcity of money, lack of business planning skills, limited understanding of market research, and a desire or need to be involved in entrepreneurial activity. Ideally, customers will own computers and have access to the Internet; however, the books are equally effective using only a pencil and calculator. To entice these customers to purchase, Macrolink will need to provide affordable, upbeat, and safe ways for all individuals to participate in the business planning process, with different options available for them to advance at their own pace.

Macrolink's primary customers will include the *eleven million Canadian and American entrepreneurs* engaged in starting businesses.

Link: Download a free Profile of Customers Worksheet at **www. riskbuster.com/worksheet/32-profile-customers**

The following table shows the various customer groups.

Top Priority	Second Priority	Third Priority
1 Million Workforce-Age People Starting Businesses in Canada, Male and Female	Economic and Enterprise Development Agencies in Canada and USA	18 Million Non-Employer Business Owners in Canada and USA
10 Million Workforce-Age People Starting Businesses in USA, Male and Female	Independent Distributors, Bookstores, Colleges and Libraries, Chains That Sell Books	Workforce-Age People Starting Businesses Not in Canada or USA

Actions

1. Revisit Steps 20 (see page 92) and 29 (see page 110) and fine-tune your description of your customers, with attention to the following questions:

   - Who influences the buying decisions?
   - How much will customers pay for your products and services?
   - What will your average sale be?
   - How are the key competitors positioned in the mind of the customers?
   - How sensitive are the buyers to pricing differences?
   - What motivates customers to buy your products and services?

2. To complete this Element, you will need to:

   - Gather information from your primary and secondary sources.

- Identify your customers' demographic profile, including their age, gender, marital status, household location, family size and description, earnings, disposable income, education level, occupation, cultural background, etc.

- Identify your customers' psychographic profile, including their lifestyle, their needs, their interests, and their purchasing habits.

- Determine and list your customers' principal buying motives.

- Identify who influences the buying decisions.

- From your research, state what the customer will pay for your products and services.

- Decide and communicate what the average sale will be.

- Describe how customers perceive the key competitors.

- Determine how sensitive buyers are to pricing differences.

Step 39: Analyze Your Competitors and Differentiate

MUST HAVE	RECOMMENDED	NICE TO HAVE

Develop a profile of your competitors and differentiate your business from them. In order to differentiate your business from competitors, you must understand their strengths and weaknesses.

Example: Competition and Differentiation

Entrepreneurs currently address their business planning requirements in a variety of ways, from ignoring the need and starting their enterprise without a business plan to hiring a consultant to create the plan for them. Starting a business without a plan is like trying to fly a jet without first taking the time to learn how to fly. For the typical owner/operator of a small or micro business, hiring a consultant to develop a business plan makes about as much sense as paying someone else to take flying lessons. In order to understand their business, most entrepreneurs should develop their own business plans.

The following options currently dominate the market: books, digital products, workshops, consulting services, and business counseling services.

Books: A variety of publications are available in the market, through bookstores and the Internet. Analysis shows prices from a low of $14.95 to a high of $69.95, with most books competing in the $20.00 to $40.00 range. Also available are a number of free publications offered by all or most financial institutions and government agencies. In the course of researching to write the *Business Planner's Toolkit*, Boudreau purchased 24 books and gathered a number of free publications from a variety of sources.

Digital Products: A number of digital business planning products are available, ranging from free to over $500. The two that currently seem to dominate the market, *Business Plan Pro* and *Bizplan Builder*, both currently sell at approximately $115 ($99USD). Boudreau has purchased and tested nine different software options and found that most do not successfully deal with both the narrative and the financial portions of the business plan. Business planning software products are either beyond the capacity of the novice, or are so streamlined that they enable the user to fabricate a relatively slick business plan without actually having to learn about their business. In an attempt to make it easy for the end user, software options typically neglect the most important benefit of business planning: to gain confidence through learning about one's business by researching the market.

Workshops: Most communities have local facilitators who provide business planning workshops at prices ranging from $350 to $1,000 per day. However, not many have specialized in business planning. Most often they are either experienced facilitators offering business planning as one of many topics, or consultants with knowledge but limited facilitation skills.

With the RoadMap™ as a foundation, Macrolink workshops not only teach participants about business planning, they also equip users with an organized approach so they know how to navigate the market research and business planning processes.

Consulting Services: It will typically cost between $30 and $100 per hour to have a consultant write a business plan for you. It can cost from $2,000 to $30,000 or more to have a consultant develop a business plan, which is simply not viable for most small or micro businesses. Macrolink will differentiate from consultants by positioning as a business planning coach for customers who wish to develop their own business plans. Macrolink will not develop business plans for customers.

Business Counseling Services: Many economic and enterprise development agencies provide free counseling services for business planners. For example, most of the Community Futures Development Corporations in rural communities across Canada employ business analysts and sometimes self-employment benefits (SEB) coordinators, whose job is to assist entrepreneurs with business planning. Most of these competitors differ from Macrolink's coaching services in that they are usually gatekeepers for either loan funds or the SEB Program.

Boudreau's marketing strategy will include inviting and encouraging counselors to become customers by using the RiskBuster Business Planning System™ and, where possible, distributing the books and digital products to their clients.

The majority of people who need business plans face the following challenges.

1. They are unfamiliar and uncomfortable with business forecasting, planning, and writing.

2. They tend to be intimidated by gatekeepers (bankers, advisors, and analysts).

3. They are unsure which of the confusing array of business planning formats to use.

4. They do not have access to a clear, effective, step-by-step business planning process.

Macrolink Business Planning solutions are different in the following ways:

1. The RoadMap™ dovetails the market research and business planning processes, enabling users to navigate from the business idea to implementation, step by step.

2. The products will transform the business planning process into a safe, manageable, learning adventure.

3. Books will be positioned in the medium-to-high price range and in the high-quality category.

4. CDs and digital downloads will be positioned in the lower price range and medium-quality category.

Actions

1. Review the market research and the results from Step 22 (see page 95).

2. List the names and locations of major competitors.

3. Compare various competitors on the basis of appearance of their business sites, the layout of their operations, number of employees, and how long they have been in business.

4. Compare products and services between different businesses.

5. Note similarities and differences in brand, features, benefits, and prices.

6. Estimate the sales or market share for each competitor.

7. Compare all competitors strengths and weaknesses.

8. Determine why customers buy from your competitors.

9. Differentiate your business from the competitors and clarify why the customer will buy from your business.

10. Develop this Element and enter it into the working copy of your business plan.

11. Save any important comparisons or survey and test results in the Appendices.

12. Tables can be used to demonstrate the comparisons and differences between competitors.

Tip: Don't bad-mouth competitors. It is far stronger to promote your strengths and benefits than to say negative things about your competitors.

Step 40: Describe How You Will Sell

MUST HAVE	RECOMMENDED	NICE TO HAVE

Determine which sales activities will best reach your customers. The methods you choose will be determined in part by your product, by your customers, and by the methods used by your competitors. This step leads to writing the Sales and Distribution Element in the Operations Section of your business plan.

Example: Sales and Distribution

The main objective of Macrolink's marketing strategy is to get distribution. During the first three years of business, the owner will self-distribute the books and digital products, and will also promote and sell through the shopping cart at the publisher's website. The publisher will do some marketing of the book via the Internet and will also publish the books on demand. This will eliminate the need to publish or stock large inventories of books until customers place orders.

Once the Macrolink website is established, the owner will approach bookstores, economic development agencies, associations and organizations in the economic development field. Boudreau will actively promote himself as a speaker and facilitator at strategic conferences. For example, Western Canadian Community Futures Development Corporations will schedule a training sessions each year.

Macrolink will sell its products and services through the following methods:

- Books sold by the publisher through its website bookstore.
- Facilitator manuals and business planning products sold directly to trainers.
- Facilitators' receiving a discount on hard-copy and digital learner materials.
- Selling products directly to book stores, retailers, and distributors.

- Co-marketing agreements established with software and business development organizations.

- Offering affordable three-hour seminars to generate book and CD sales.

- Selling books and CDs at trade shows.

Boudreau will be the salesperson for the first three years of the business.

Actions

To complete this Element, you will need to complete your analysis of the various competitors and then:

1. Identify which sales methods are being used most successfully by the competition.

2. Determine the Industry standard for getting products and services to the customers.

3. Choose which sales methods will best work for you, giving careful consideration to the amount of available time, energy, and money.

Tip: Never promise more than what you can deliver; always deliver a little more than your customer expects.

Step 41: Clarify Servicing and Guarantees

MUST HAVE	RECOMMENDED	NICE TO HAVE

Clarify the level of service you will offer and what you will promise to replace or repair. This Element consists of promises that a business person must live up to.

Servicing and Guarantees Example

Macrolink offers the following guarantee:

Your success is our success. We stand behind the quality of our products and services. If for any reason you are not completely satisfied, return all materials to us within 15 days of purchase to receive a full refund. This policy does not apply to digital products downloaded from our website; however, we will replace any defective digital products within 15 days of purchase.

The guarantee will be posted at the Macrolink website and in promotional materials.

Actions

To complete this Element you will need to complete your analysis of the various competitors and then:

1. Identify any guarantees your competitors offer with their products and services.

2. Clarify and write your customer service philosophy.

3. Describe your servicing and guarantee strategy.

4. Estimate any related costs and build them into your prices.

Step 42: Craft Your Business Image

MUST HAVE	RECOMMENDED	NICE TO HAVE

Create an effective corporate image.

Image Example

Macrolink is in business to serve entrepreneurs. Its products and services are practical, affordable, and professional. To maintain a consistently professional image, all communications, materials, and printed products maintain a consistently professional quality and tone. Customers who purchase products and services from Macrolink will receive excellent value for their investment. As the logo portrays, Macrolink is a responsible corporation that respects the environment and empowers ordinary people through learning. By Year Four, assuming continued and growing profitability, the business will begin contributing 5% of pre-tax profits to assist micro-entrepreneurs with business plan development and start-up capital. These monies will be vetted through existing not-for-profit enterprise development agencies.

Actions

To complete this Element you will need to complete your analysis of the various competitors and then:

1. Decide what kind of image your business will project.
2. Consider your likes and dislikes and how you wish your business to be perceived in the marketplace.
3. Write a description of your business image.

Step 43: Develop Advertising and Promotion

MUST HAVE	RECOMMENDED	NICE TO HAVE

Determine the most effective approaches, tools and methods to increase your customers' awareness of your products and services.

Ad Specialties	Décor	Newsletters
Advertising Services	Demonstrations	Newspaper Ads
Answering Machine	Direct Mail	Parking Meter Ads
Articles	Directories	Per Inquiry Ads
Audiocassettes	Distributors	Personal Contact
Balloons	Donations	Placemats
Billboards	Door Hangers	Postcards
Birthday Cards	E-Bulletin Boards	Posters
Books	Exhibits	Public Speaking
Booths (displays)	Fairs	Publicity
Brochures	Fax Broadcast	Radio Spots
Bulletin Boards	Feature Stories	Recorded Messages
Business Cards	Fixtures	Reports
Business Card Ads	Fliers	Restroom Ads
Calendar Listings	Fund Raisers	Sandwich Signs
Canvassing	Gift Certificates	Seminars
Card Decks	Gifts	Signs
Catalogues	Group Mailings	Special Events
Celebrities	Info-Lines	Sponsorships
Centers of Influence	Inserts	Statement Stuffers
Clinics	Lighting	Surveys
Co-op Mailings or Ads	Personal Letters	T-Shirt Ads
Color Schemes	Listings	Television
Columns	Magazine Ads	Telemarketing
Contests	Matchbooks	Trade Shows
Coupons	Name Tags	TV Guides
Courses	Theatre Ads	Uniforms
Customer Appreciation	News Releases	Vanity Radio

Advertising and Promotion Example

As a part of the package price for publishing the book, the publisher will offer the book for sale through its website. The publisher package also includes notifying Amazon.com, Borders.com, Barnes & Noble, Chapters.Indigo, Baker & Taylor distributors, Bowker's Books-in-Print, BookData UK and PubStock.

In addition to the publisher's marketing, the owner will actively market and promote Macrolink products and services. Each product or service will include ads or coupons for other Macrolink products and services. In this way, the marketing will be fully integrated, creating opportunities for existing customers to purchase other products and services from Macrolink. All materials will advertise the website.

The business will convey a consistent message and build a high profile by:

- Producing quality marketing materials for products and services (business cards, brochures, postcards, and posters) that drive traffic to the website.

- Providing affordable business planning workshops and seminars.

- Hosting websites at various strategic domains currently held by Macrolink: **riskbuster.com, bp99.com, macrolink.ca**.

- Placing advertisements for specific products and services in strategic publications.

- Publishing and delivering a free, opt-in monthly e-zine for entrepreneurs.

- Writing articles on business planning and related topics for e-zines and magazines.

- Maintaining a professional image on all communications, products, and documents.

- Hosting display booths at key tradeshows in the target Industry sectors.

Actions

To complete this Element you will need to analyse the various competitors and then:

1. Determine the Industry standard as to the percentage of revenue put towards advertising and marketing.

2. Establish which methods within your means will enable you to achieve your goals.

3. Develop a detailed 12-month advertising and promotion plan and budget (a Worksheet download link is provided at the bottom of this page).

4. Brainstorm how your business can get free publicity or how you can partner with other businesses or agencies to conserve costs.

5. Include the detailed budget in the Appendices Section of your business plan.

6. Identify areas needing further market research and set goals to carry it out.

7. Develop a summary of your advertising, promotion, and publicity plan for this Element.

8. Define as many components of your marketing package as you can, with attention to your business graphics, logo design, business cards, letterhead, packaging, signs, advertising style, methods of sales, telephone use, service, and physical surroundings.

Link: Download a free Advertising and Promotion Plan Checklist
www.riskbuster.com/worksheet/64-advertising-and-promotion-plan-checklist

---

Step 44: Present Prices and Pricing Strategy

MUST HAVE	RECOMMENDED	NICE TO HAVE

Set prices for your products and services. In order to set prices you must first be clear about costs.

There are at least three ways to set your prices. To establish prices for your products and services, you might employ all three methods: pricing to market, pricing to cost, and break-even pricing.

Pricing to Market

Pricing to market means setting your prices according to the competitive market prices. Using this method will restrict you to finding your profit through efficiencies and savings on your costs. Some types of business will compel you to set your prices to market.

Pricing to Cost

Pricing to cost means determining your cost to make your product or service, adding on your desired profit margin, and adding the two amounts together in order to arrive at your price. Another way to state this is to determine your cost of goods sold, identify the Industry standard mark-up for the product or service, and then add the two together to create your price.

Break-Even Pricing

Break-even pricing means determining how much you need for your business to break-even overall and then setting your product and service prices to break even and earn a profit.

Tip: If you are working in a high-risk Industry or business, be sure to match the percentage of profit to the level of risk. High risk should equal a higher amount of profit. To ignore this is to invite financial disaster at some point in the future.

Things to Consider when Setting Prices

1. How price sensitive are your customers?

2. Do your customers decide to buy based on price or on other characteristics such as quality, location, or convenience?

3. What is the cost of producing your products or services?

4. What are your competitors' prices for similar products or services?

5. How many units do you have to sell in order to break-even or earn a profit?

6. What are the Industry standard mark-ups or margins for your product or service?

7. What discount rates will you offer for bulk purchases?

8. How much will your customer pay for your product or service?

9. What is the relationship of supply to demand?

10. What are the consumer buying trends?

11. What is your level of risk?

12. What is your desired profit margin?

13. What are your personal and corporate financial goals?

Establishing Your Pricing Strategy

Your first concern will be to determine whether your product or service can live in the marketplace. In other words, can you hope to sell it for enough to pay your bills, survive, and earn a small profit? Unless you are already financially independent, one of your top priorities should be to ensure that the business can earn a profit.

Beyond the first priority of establishing viability, a number of other concerns enable you to chart your course in regard to setting pricing objectives. The list on the following page provides a few pricing considerations to help you get started.

1. What are your desired timelines to become established in the market?

2. Do you wish to sell more products or services for lower profits or fewer products or services for higher profits?

3. Will you initiate price wars by selling at prices lower than your competitors?

4. Do you have the resources to survive a prolonged price war, or do your competitors have deeper pockets?

5. Do you have control over or flexibility with your product and service costs?

6. Do you have control over or flexibility with your prices to customers?

7. Are there existing Industry standard markup percentages you must adhere to?

8. What levels of the distribution will you occupy? Will you be a manufacturer, a wholesaler, a distributor, or a retailer?

9. What image will your price create with your customers?

Pricing Strategy Example

Macrolink pricing strategy is to offer clients practical and affordable business planning solutions.

Since 2001, the owner has surveyed more than 500 entrepreneurs. Those surveyed include individual male and female adults from 20 to 54 years old who demonstrated an interest in starting a business. Feedback indicates that 90% of those surveyed will pay between $29 and $99 for business planning solutions. The following list shows the 12 units and prices used to forecast sales for the first three years of operation for the business.

Product or Service Unit	Cost of Goods Sold	Customer Unit Price
1. Books-Publisher-Retail	14.63	36.58
2. Books-Publisher-Bookstores	14.63	21.95
3. Books-Publisher-Distributor	14.63	18.29
4. Books-Owner-Retail	14.19	36.58
5. CD-Retail	5.00	29.50
6. CD-Distributors	5.00	29.50
7. Digital Downloads Retail	5.00	29.50
8. Half-Day Workshops		350.00
9. Full-Day Workshops		495.00
10. Seminars for Individuals		49.00
11. Facilitator Manuals	50.00	99.95
12. Consulting and Coaching Hours		40.00

Notes to Pricing
1. All prices are in US dollars.
2. Cost of Goods Sold (COGS) is estimated at the highest rate (retail, one book on demand) for all book sales.
3. COGS are entered at the highest cost of production ($5 per CD), although prices will be less for volume purchases.

Link: Download a free Pricing Worksheet from the website at **www.riskbuster.com/worksheet/33-pricing**

Tip: In situations where your service will include product, keep them as separate units. For example, my training service might be accompanied by the sale of books and CDs as separate units. Keeping each unit separate offers more flexibility in forecasting, in marketing and in selling your products and services.

Actions

To complete this Element you will need to complete your analysis of competitor prices, gather all information related to your costs and then:

1. Familiarize yourself with the three methods of pricing, including pricing to market, pricing to costs, and break-even pricing. Take all three methods into consideration in order to determine where to position your product or service.

2. You can begin the process by setting your prices to market, but it is important to understand that you must confirm viability by completing the Financial Section and comparing the other two methods: pricing to your costs and pricing to your break-even. You can only truly determine whether or not your pricing strategy works by completing your financial projections; then you will be able to see the overall impact on the bottom line in your projected income statement.

3. Using the information gathered for your competitive analysis, develop a table to compare the competitor's prices.

4. Create a bottom-up or cost-based price for each product or service. You can use the Worksheet following this list or the pricing Worksheet in the Biz4Caster™.

5. Write a summary of your pricing strategy in this Element and include relevant detail in the Appendices.

6. Use pricing notes to clarify any potentially confusing points for your reader. Make notes of any assumptions or key information on which you have based your estimates.

WORKSHEET: PRICING				
Product and Service Units	*Supplier Cost (COGS)**	*Price to Customer Input*	*Year Two % Growth*	*Year Three % Growth*
1.				
2.				

Note: Products will always have a Cost of Goods Sold, while services typically do not *unless* they are subcontracted.

Step 45: Develop a Marketing Action Plan

MUST HAVE	RECOMMENDED	NICE TO HAVE

Plan a strategy for marketing your products and services.

Marketing Action Plan Example

OBJECTIVES AND GOALS	WHO	COST
1. Build a website at **www.riskbuster.com** • Website and shopping cart	Owner Sys Admin	$5,000
2. Secure legal rights and develop logos for domains and names • Brand **www.riskbuster.com**	Owner Sys Admin	2,000
3. Publish book • Establish marketing, schedule, and book launch	Owner Publisher	2,000
4. Develop, schedule, and organize business planning seminars • Organize seminars for areas demonstrating demand	Owner	1,000
5. Proactively seek publicity • Develop press releases; email and fax to selected media • Write and submit business planning articles	Owner	100
6. Design integrated materials that drive traffic to the website(s) • Build marketing copy into each product package • Design and publish brochures	Owner Designer	2,500

OBJECTIVES AND GOALS	WHO	COST
7. Design and place product ads in strategic publications • Identify various target publications, research costs, run tests	Owner	2,000
8. Market owner and author as speaker or facilitator for conferences • Develop marketing materials and copy • Actively seek engagements by contacting conference organizers	Owner	4,400
9. Post content, free products, and functions that draw traffic to the website, including: • Free e-zine for entrepreneurs • Archived articles on business planning related topics • Searchable glossary of business terms • Free downloadable business planning Shell™ • Sample business plans • Downloadable video "how-to" clips (e.g. how to do a cash flow)	Owner	
Total Marketing Budget		$19,000

Actions

1. Review market research that you consider to be helpful in creating your Marketing Action Plan.

2. Copy the Advertising and Promotion Element into a separate file and use it as a benchmark from which to build your Marketing Action Plan.

3. Build your list of Marketing Objectives and arrange them chronologically, in the order they will happen.

4. Develop a brief list of action goals for each objective.

5. Estimate a budget for each of the components of your Marketing Action Plan. This can be done in a spreadsheet either in the cash flow projection or separately; ultimately these costs must be put into your cash flow projection.

6. Option: Go back and reorganize your Advertising and Promotion Element to be more consistent with your Marketing Action Plan.

WORKSHEET: MARKETING ACTION PLAN		
Objectives and Goals	*Who*	*Budget*
1.		
2.		
3.		
4.		
5.		
6.		
7.		
Total Marketing Budget		

Link: Download a free Marketing Action Plan Worksheet at **www.riskbuster.com/worksheet/34-marketing-action-plan**

Organize Your Operations Section

Provide your reader with an understanding of how your operations will run.

Here are the business plan Elements in this Section and the corresponding RoadMap™ steps:

Business Plan Element	RoadMap™ Steps
Description of the Operation	46
Equipment and Methods	47
Materials and Supplies	48
Insurance	49
Management	50
Professional Services	51
Employees and Contractors	52
Operational Action Plan	53

Read the Operations Section of the Macrolink Business Plan to get a sense of what you are trying to achieve in this Section.

Link: Download the Macrolink Business Plan from the website at **www.riskbuster.com/content/business-plan**

Step 46: Describe Your Operation

MUST HAVE	RECOMMENDED	NICE TO HAVE

Clarify how and where your business will operate.

Description of the Operation Example

Macrolink is a home-based company licensed in the city of Prince George, British Columbia. The owner outsources the core functions of bookkeeping, technical services, and product production. No walk-in traffic is necessary, as all products and services are produced and provided off site.

Products and services will be provided as follows:

- Books will be published on-demand at the publisher's location. Boudreau will have the option of purchasing higher volumes of books at discounted rates. Storage facilities will be rented as needed to house products.

- CD production will be outsourced. Storage space will be rented as needed, keeping overhead low.

- Facilitator manuals are anticipated to be much lower volume and will initially be produced by the owner. If demand increases beyond the capacity of the home office, the owner will either outsource the production of the manuals to a local print shop or publish them through the publisher.

- Workshops, seminars and consulting services will be provided at either the customer's location or other suitable facilities, to be rented as needed to provide these services.

The owner uses a portable notebook computer and is able to work from any location that has an Internet connection.

Actions

When making decisions about your business location, consider cost, customer convenience, and your needs and capabilities.

To complete this Element you will need to complete your analysis of competitor locations, gather all information related to your business location and then:

1. Decide whether to rent or lease office space or to operate from your home.

2. Check out all legal aspects related to the chosen location, including zoning, bylaws, building regulations, building codes, agreements with owners, health and fire inspections, and permits.

Tip: Be careful about locking into long-term leases with percentage-of-sales clauses. Huge success in your business can trigger massive lease payments.

Tip: This Element can be effective as text, but pictures can bring it to life. Pictures can be helpful to communicate about parts of your business that are complex or unfamiliar to the readers of your business plan. For example, it might be helpful to show a picture of a facility or a piece of equipment rather than trying to describe it.

Step 47: List Equipment and Methods

MUST HAVE	RECOMMENDED	NICE TO HAVE

Determine your equipment needs and methods for meeting those needs

Example: Equipment and Methods

The Macrolink home office is equipped with enough office furniture to meet business needs for the first few years of operation. Research and development costs for writing the books and creating the digital products, estimated to be in excess of $40,000, are not included in the opening balance sheet.

EQUIPMENT LIST			
Item	*Source*	*Credit Details*	*Cost*
Satellite Notebook	Boudreau	Owner Contribution	$1,800
HP Inkjet 2200	Boudreau	Owner Contribution	200
Brother IntelliFAX 2800	Boudreau	Owner Contribution	100
Jeep Cherokee	Boudreau	Owner Contribution	15,000
Satellite 330 Laptop	Boudreau	Owner Contribution	300
M3 Presenter	Boudreau	Owner Contribution	200
TOTAL			$17,600.00

Actions

1. To complete this Element you will need to gather information related to all equipment required to operate as well as the costs and the methods used to acquire the items (purchase, rent, or lease).

2. Determine your operational equipment requirements, costs, and methods.

3. Determine your office furnishings and supply requirements, costs, and methods. For example, filing cabinets, in-out file baskets or trays, desks, lamps, chairs, shelving, bookcases, staplers, hole punches, file folders, dividers, labels, paper clips, binders, invoice and receipt forms, pens, pencils, paper, telephone message forms, magazine storage boxes, etc.

4. Determine your business equipment requirements, costs, and methods. For example, telephone (office, cell), answering machine, personal computers, notebooks, modems, printers, fax machine, photocopier, etc.

WORKSHEET: EQUIPMENT LIST			
Item	*Source*	*Credit Details*	*Cost*
TOTAL			

Link: Download a free Equipment and Methods Worksheet at **www.riskbuster.com/worksheet/35-equipment-list**

Step 48: Source Materials and Supplies

MUST HAVE	RECOMMENDED	NICE TO HAVE

Determine what supplies and materials you will require to create your product or service, and sources for each. This will be a critical step toward completing the Financial Section of your business plan.

Example: Materials and Supplies

The publisher provides a detailed list of costs for books, based on the number of pages and the quantities purchased. To limit the risk and control overhead, the owner will purchase higher quantities of books only as demand dictates.

CDs will be created by an established replication service from the Vancouver area.

For all training and trainer resources, supplies and materials will be purchased from local office suppliers. All bulk photocopying is done at highly competitive rates by a local provider, located only a few minutes from the Macrolink office.

Actions

To complete this Element you will need to gather all information from different suppliers and compare their literature and terms, then:

1. Consider your financial ability and how it fits with the supplier terms.

2. Ensure that you can meet your customer obligations and stay on top of inventory costs.

3. In the case of human resource suppliers, consider subcontracting and establishing a 15 or 30-day payment policy to give yourself room to collect from clients before having to pay your resources.

4. Decide which suppliers you will use. If possible, get a letter of commitment from them or complete their credit application and open an account.

5. Make a list of your materials, supplies and sources.

MATERIALS AND SUPPLIES TABLE			
Supplier	*Availability*	*Credit Terms*	*Policies*

Link: Download a free Materials and Supplies Worksheet at **www.riskbuster.com/worksheet/36-materials-and-supplies**

Tip: A bulleted or numbered list can be effective for this Element. As well, the preceding table might provide an appropriate way to communicate this Element.

Step 49: Identify and Control Your Risks

MUST HAVE	RECOMMENDED	NICE TO HAVE

Assess threats to your business and determine how you will manage risk.

As you researched to get to this stage, you undoubtedly became more aware of the risks. Now is the time to take an open-minded look at which threats you might encounter and to develop your strategies for mitigating risk. Business and life are risky; there's no getting away from that. Your goal with this Element is to chart a path you can live comfortably with. Here are some of the demons you might face–feel free to add a few of your own.

POTENTIAL THREATS AND MITIGATION STRATEGIES	
Threats	*Possible Mitigation*
Employee or Contractor Disputes	Do your due diligence before hiring or signing contracts; develop clear agreements and ensure you live up to your end of those agreements.
Health and Safety	Know the regulations, be vigilant for liabilities, create and distribute policies and procedures, and buy the appropriate insurance(s).
Personal Safety	Be aware of areas within your operations where personal safety could become an issue. Provide ongoing education for your employees about risky areas and suggest safe practices. Develop and publicize standards and policies for all nature of harassment. Make it part of your mission to create a working environment free from discomfort, intimidation, or offensive acts.

Threats	*Possible Mitigation*
Fatigue and Burnout	Enter a type of business that you enjoy and one that doesn't keep you stressed and fatigued. Youthful vigor has pulled me through many 20-hour days and too many 100+ hour work weeks. Being committed to your business is a good thing until it begins to take a toll on your health. Often it's when the business gets into trouble that an owner starts slugging it out for long hours, days, or weeks on end. The scariest thing about burnout is that it creeps up on you. In my case, it wasn't until long after the business crises that I fully realized how thoroughly drained I was. Stay fit, exercise regularly, eat well, and get enough sleep and play. Learn and pay attention to the signs of burnout and make adjustments when it hits.
Lawsuits or Fines	Operate in a spirit of fairness; document everything; develop and use procedures for documenting and dealing with critical incidents.
Fire and Emergency	Create escape procedures, place them in visible locations, research the relevant regulations, train staff and contractors, and buy insurance.
Facilities and Equipment	Facilities bring with them a host of threats, from fire and theft to health and safety issues. The insurance Industry provides coverage for just about every occasion. It is possible to spend all of your would be profits on insurance. You must determine your level of risk and purchase the right amount of insurance.
Computers, Website and Technology	Today's workplace is highly dependent on technology. For the most part, if our computer, email, website or file server misses a beat, we cannot work. This means taking safety and security seriously from the ground up. Use quality equipment and back-up everything regularly. Use a reputable Internet service provider and a level of technical support appropriate to your need.

Threats	*Possible Mitigation*
Intangible Properties, Copyright and Trademark Protection	The world of intangible properties is undergoing dramatic changes as businesses and governments struggle to embrace issues globally. This area, as witnessed by the music Industry, is a hotbed of theft, wrongdoing, and litigation. Your best mitigation is to engage a competent IP lawyer and play by the rules for each jurisdiction you operate in. Recognize there are areas in the world where copyright and trademark have no substance whatsoever.
Sales Shortfall	Your business plan is only as strong as your confidence in your sales projections. If you are not confident in your ability to meet the sales projected in your business plan, redo the projections until you are. New business start-ups tend to be too optimistic in projecting sales. Keep your projections as comfortably low as you can. It is healthy to have a certain amount of money set aside (contingency) to see you through if sales fall short.
Product or Service Quality	When it comes to dealing with customers, a business owner is fully responsible to maintain product or service quality. There may be many others in the supply line who have control over aspects of the quality, but you are accountable to your customer. Develop a quality statement and live up to it.
Supply	A number of factors can create interruptions in your supply of goods or services. It is important that you assess these factors and prepare alternative plans to provide your product or service. The entire world runs on supply and demand. If your supply chain is rife with threats, perhaps you need to consider alternates. The dynamics are very different for a simple service business where you, the owner, provide the service. Any supply problems are then directly related to your ability to provide the service.

Threats	*Possible Mitigation*
Competitor Reaction	How will your competitors react to your entry into business? If you think a competitor will lower prices, can you withstand a protracted price war? Sometimes an Industry is large enough, or a business differentiated enough, that competition is not a big concern. Other situations require going head to head with existing businesses. Whatever the situation, the onus will be on you to stay ahead of your competitors.
Politics	Ah, politics, the oldest prostitution! You will not escape politics; they are pervasive, ever-changing and powerful. The time to assess and understand the politics affecting your business is during the start-up stage. How is your crystal ball working? Educate yourself on the politics of your business, determine the level of risk and then decide whether you can live comfortably with those risks. Once you are in business, stay involved; keep a thumb on the pulse of your Industry and your business.
Legal and Regulatory	The onus is on you to know the laws and regulations affecting your business. Ignorance is not a viable defense. As with politics, pre-start-up is the time to assess and determine whether you can live with the laws and regulations governing your business. Know the rules and stay on top of changes.

Threats	*Possible Mitigation*
Cash Flow Shortfall	Cash flow is the lifeblood of your business. Stop the cash flow and your business quickly dies. From opening day onward you are responsible to orchestrate a balance between revenues and expenses. This will entail making sales, collecting receivables, purchasing supplies, maintaining equipment, paying expenses and hopefully paying yourself. There are a few things you can do to stack the cards in your favor. Foster a positive credit rating, develop a solid relationship with your banker, maintain access to an operating loan, keep headroom on your credit cards, pay expenses promptly to avoid interest charges, open and use trade accounts where appropriate, and regularly save money to build up a contingency fund.
Bad Debts	Some types of business require that you extend credit to customers. For example, many government contracts tend to pay two to three months after a service is provided. If it's the Industry standard, you will have to conform in order to remain competitive. If the Industry standard is to be paid cash, stick to it. If there is no compelling reason to extend credit, don't. Limit the amount of credit you extend to customers and stay on top of your receivables. If you detect a customer slipping away from you, communicate directly with him or her.

WORKSHEET: THREATS AND MITIGATION	
Threats	*Possible Mitigation*

Actions

To complete this Element you will need to determine your facility, equipment and liability risk, then:

1. Review your market research with an eye on threats to your business.

2. Using the blank Threats and Mitigation Worksheet on the preceding page as your model, brainstorm and prioritize a list of risks to your business.

3. List your strategies to mitigate each risk or threat. If necessary, do more research.

4. Contact a trusted or referred insurance agent to determine your insurance needs.

Some of your threats will require insurance. The list of different types of insurance is endless. A few types of insurance you may want to consider are: house or business premises, vehicle, liability, inventory, business interruption, disability, partnership, and loan insurance.

Link: Download a free Threats and Mitigation Worksheet at **www. riskbuster.com/worksheet/37-threats-and-mitigation**

Tip: Do your customers use the Internet? If so, consider testing the web-based survey applications at **www.zoomerang.com** or **www.surveymonkey.com**.

Step 50: Describe Your Management Team

MUST HAVE	RECOMMENDED	NICE TO HAVE

Determine who will manage your business and describe your Management Team.

Because management is such a critical aspect of any business, you will want to put careful thought into this Element. If you are hiring a manager, you will need to consider a number of key points within your business planning process:

- Establish job descriptions and hiring criteria.

- Identify the manager's roles and responsibilities.

- Determine what training you will provide for a manager.

- Assess Industry standards and establish a budget for salary and training.

- Consider what rewards and recognition you will establish for employees.

In my case, this was an easy Element because I am the chief cook and bottle washer–end of story. My biography already exists in the owner Element of the Business Concept Section. There was nothing to be gained by replicating what has been written there, so I chose to elaborate on my history as a business manager.

Example: Management Team

Dan Boudreau, owner, will manage the business. Boudreau has owned and managed five small businesses in the past 24 years. He will manage the company until it grows to the point that it can sustain an office manager or operations manager, at which time job descriptions and hiring criteria will be developed. Management salary will be set at $180 per day until the business can sustain a higher rate. More information on the owner is in Appendix 6.1.

Action

To complete this Element you will need to identify your own strengths and weaknesses, then:

1. Determine whether or not you will manage the business yourself.

2. Identify what training you or your manager will require.

3. Forecast all management-related salaries and training costs.

4. If you are the only person working in the business and you have already provided your background information in the applicant Element, you need only to focus in this Element on your training needs and strengths that were not highlighted there.

Tip: If you're developing a business plan for a small or micro business, consider eliminating this Element and expanding your biography in Step 34 (see page 130) to include your management skills.

Tip: There is one practice you will want to follow when dealing with professionals: always prepare yourself by clarifying in advance what you want them to do for you. The more you can organize your thoughts prior to meeting with lawyers, bankers, or accountants, the less time it will take for them to understand and carry out your requests. More importantly, it will cost you less. An ounce of preparation is worth a pound of profit.

Step 51: Select Your Professionals

MUST HAVE	RECOMMENDED	NICE TO HAVE

Research and select your professional service providers and describe your professional services.

At a minimum you will want to consider the following professionals for your team: lawyer, accountant, bookkeeper, Industry expert, business advisor, and graphics designer.

Selecting Professionals

Take some time to research and select your professional team. You may be getting married for a long time, assuming your business will be successful. Changing professionals can be disruptive and costly.

Questions to Ask Your Banker

1. What services do you provide for small business?

2. Under what circumstances would you lend money to a new business?

3. What interest rate and what fees would I pay on a term loan or an operating loan?

4. What are your policies regarding to security and collateral?

5. When lending to a small business, what do you consider to be the minimum and ideal percentage of owner equity or investment?

6. What is your experience or impression of the business (restaurants, tourism, service, etc.)?

7. What size of loans do you make the decisions on before having to refer the package to a higher authority?

Questions to Ask Your Accountant

1. Describe your services for small business.

2. What are your rates for accounting? What are your rates for bookkeeping?

3. For a business of my type and size, what are the annual accounting and bookkeeping costs?

4. Can you tell me how much it would cost to set up my chart of accounts?

5. If necessary, would you be able to prepare financial projections for my business?

6. What accounting software do you use? Do you use email?

7. What are your payment terms?

8. Who would you recommend as a banker or lawyer for a business like mine?

Questions to Ask Your Lawyer

1. Please describe your services for small business.

2. Can you tell me what area of law you focus on (seeking experience with corporate and contract law).

3. What are your hourly rates?

4. Can you tell how much it will cost to set up my proprietorship, corporation, etc.?

5. What word processing software do you use?

6. If necessary, can I communicate with you via email?

7. What are your payment terms?

8. Who would you recommend as an accountant for a business like mine?

Questions to Ask Your Bookkeeper

1. Please describe your services for small business.

2. Do you have the ability to provide monthly draft financial statements?

3. How many and what types of small businesses do you currently provide bookkeeping services for? Can you provide me with three references?

4. What training or background do you have as a bookkeeper?

5. How many years' experience do you have providing bookkeeping services?

6. What equipment do you currently have in your office, and what accounting software do you use?

7. If necessary, can I communicate with you via email?

8. What are your hourly rates?

9. What are your payment terms?

Example: Professional Services

> Accounting, legal, and insurance will be outsourced from established businesses.

Action

To complete this Element you will need to do some networking to get name referrals; then:

1. Prepare in advance by determining what you wish to learn from each professional.

2. Within the business network in your area, ask for names of recommended professionals.

3. Contact the professionals you wish to consider and arrange a meeting to discuss your needs.

4. Decide which advisors you will engage and enter their information in the table below.

WORKSHEET: PROFESSIONAL SERVICES			
Specialty	*Name*	*Company*	*Tel/Fax/Email*
Accountant			
Lawyer			

Link: Download a free Professional Services Worksheet at **www. riskbuster.com/worksheet/38-professional-services**

Step 52: Determine Labor Requirements

MUST HAVE	RECOMMENDED	NICE TO HAVE

Plan and describe how many employees and contractors you will need for your first year in business.

In completing this process, you will want to consider the following:

- Your skills and the skills required for your business.
- Your experience and credibility for the products or services you plan to provide.
- Whether to employ or subcontract–consider the Industry standard.
- How many employees or contractors you will engage and what rates you will pay them.

Example: Employees and Contractors

The owner will do all the operations work until demand for products and services increases to the point that extra help is required. Staff will be engaged as needed. Initially, the organization will contract with a part-time systems administrator and a part-time bookkeeper.

Tip: Your labor requirements, whether employee or contract, are driven by the amount of product or service you provide to your customers. It is critical that you compare this to your projected sales to ensure consistency with the fluctuations in your sales forecast. For example, your labor projections would increase commensurate with a growth in sales. If for some reason this is not the case, you should provide an explanation for your reader.

Actions

To complete this Element you will need to determine how much of the required work you will perform yourself; then:

1. Determine the amount of product or service you can create and deliver by yourself.

2. Identify areas of knowledge or skill you require (e.g., bookkeeping).

3. Determine whether you will employ or subcontract the additional help.

4. Research and clarify hourly or day rates for each position and ensure the availability of each type of worker.

5. Use the 6-month Labor Projections Worksheet on the following page as a starting point. Create a 12-month table in which to build a first-year projection of work days for each employee or subcontractor. Each row is split horizontally to allow for entry of the number of hours in the top half and the total dollar amounts in the bottom half.

6. Here is the process for projecting the amount of wages for each worker:

   a. Determine what you will use as a unit of pay for employees (monthly, daily, hourly, etc.).

   b. Calculate how much you will pay each employee per unit, not including the payroll burden (Pension Plan, Employment Insurance, Holiday Pay and Workers' Compensation).

   c. Estimate the number of units each person will work for each of the first twelve months of business operation.

   d. Multiply the number of units each month times the unit rate to arrive at the total labor projection for each worker for each month.

Tip: Although the following table is for 6 months, create your detailed labor projection for the first 12 months of your business operation or financial scenario.

Worksheet: Labor Projections

POSITION	UNIT RATE	1	2	3	4	5	6	TOTAL
Owner/Manager								
Employee 1								
Employee 2								
Subcontractor 1								
Subcontractor 2								
TOTAL								

Link: Download a free Labor Projections Worksheet from **www. riskbuster.com/worksheet/39-labor-projections**

Step 53: Develop Your Operational Action Plan

MUST HAVE	RECOMMENDED	NICE TO HAVE

Develop an Action Plan to implement your short and long-range operational goals.

In some cases it is difficult to determine whether a goal should fall into this Element or the Marketing Action Plan in the Marketing Section of your business plan. In my case, for example, which Element should house a task such as "building a website" or "providing a seminar"? I decided to leave the website production in the Marketing Section and to include the production of the seminar here. The key is to compare the two action plans in order to avoid duplication or repetitiveness.

Example: Operational Action Plan

The main actions required are:

- Complete and publish the books by July 2009
- Establish a website with a shopping cart by August 2009
- Develop the digital products by September 2009

Actions

To prepare yourself to complete this Element, first go back and review your Strategic Plan and Goals in the Business Concept Section, your Marketing Action Plan in the Marketing Section, and all Elements of this, the Operations Section—then develop your Operational Action Plan with attention to the following categories:

1. Setup of your premises and facilities.

2. Purchase and setup of equipment.

3. Purchase of materials and supplies.

4. Steps required for mitigating potential risks.

5. Engagement of management, professionals, employees, or contractors.

WORKSHEET: OPERATIONAL ACTION PLAN	
Goal	*Timelines*
1.	
2.	
3.	
4.	
5.	

Link: Download a free Operational Action Plan Worksheet at **www.riskbuster.com/worksheet/40-operational-action-plan**

Tip: You can let your imagination soar, but be very careful not to scare off your reader by dwelling on wildly unrealistic long range plans.

Tip: Unless there is an advantage for doing so, it can be problematic to put goals with deadlines into your Operational Action Plan. This is because the plan quickly becomes outdated, necessitating continuous updating to remain accurate. Although you will need timelines for internal planning purposes, it can be less complicated to leave the timelines out of this Element if the plan is to be viewed by anyone outside the business.

Forecast Your Financial Section

The purpose of this Section is to determine if your business will make money.

Here are the business plan Elements in this Section and the corresponding RoadMap™ steps:

Business Plan Element	RoadMap™ Steps
Sales Forecast	54
Explanation of Projections	55
Market Share	56
Cost of Goods Sold	57
Labor Projections	58
Cash Flow Forecast	59
Projected Income Statement	60
Break-Even Analysis	61
Pro Forma Balance Sheet	62
Startup Expenses	63
Uses and Sources of Funds	64

Read the Financial Section of the Macrolink Business Plan to get a sense of what you are trying to achieve in this Section.

A Brief Introduction to Financials and Forecasting

It is important to understand that the Financial Section of your business plan is not just for the gatekeeper, it's also for you. It is an opportunity to learn how money flows in and out of your business.

As mentioned at the beginning of this 99-step process, your business plan consists of three main parts: narrative, financial, and supporting information.

In building your Financial Section, it's critical that you understand that you are forecasting, not accounting. The difference between forecasting and accounting is illustrated in the following table:

DIFFERENCE BETWEEN FORECASTING AND ACCOUNTING	
Forecasting ...	*Accounting ...*
■ Is an educated guess at future scenarios	■ Is a detailed compilation of past transactions
■ Happens before the period of business	■ Happens after the period of business
■ Provides an approximate picture of the future	■ Provides an accurate record of past business
■ Relies on assumptions and unknowns	■ Relies on precise records and receipts
■ Is best done by you	■ Is best done by an accountant

Link: Download your free bonus copy of the RiskBuster Business Planner™ at **www.riskbuster.com/RiskBusterBook**

Step 54: Forecast Your Sales

MUST HAVE	RECOMMENDED	NICE TO HAVE

Estimate the sales or revenue your business will capture.

Forecasting for Businesses with Many Products

Here are a few suggestions to help you create a reliable sales forecast.

1. You can project sales by groups of products or by product lines to reduce the number of line items in your sales forecast.

2. You can get away from projecting by product by using the average sale as your unit. For example, if your market research reveals that three out of every ten visitors to your business will spend an average of $50 on your products or services, you can use this as your unit and project sales based on the expected number of visitors.

3. After determining your break-even point, you can base your sales projection on the average sales per day. For example, take $500 per day times 6 days per week–followed by adjustments for holidays and special occasions–and you can eventually arrive at a meaningful sales forecast.

Tip: Forecast your sales conservatively. Avoid pie-in-the-sky projections. Forecasting your sales at a lower rate than you think possible will enable you to have more confidence in your projections.

Tip: If your forecast makes you uncomfortable, imagine how your banker will feel about it. Adjust your estimates until you are comfortable with them.

Example: Sales Forecast Summary

Units	Prices	Yr 1 Units	Yr 1 Sales
Books-Publisher-Retail	$36.58	385	$ 14,083
Books-Publisher-Bookstores	21.95	260	5,707
Books-Publisher-Distributor	18.29	140	2,561
Books-Owner-Retail	36.59	545	19,942
CD-Retail	29.50	159	4,691
CD-Distributors	29.50	180	5,310
Digital Downloads Retail	29.50	260	7,670
Half-Day Workshops	350.00	6	2,100
Full-Day Workshops	495.00	24	11,880
Seminars for Individuals	49.00	100	4,900
Total Sales			$128,243
Gross Profit Margin Percentage			82.13%
COGS Percentage			17.87%

Actions

To complete this Element you will need to have completed most of your primary and secondary market research. Your basic blocks for building your sales forecast are your product and service units and the corresponding unit prices (created in Step 44 on page 152).

If you are using the Biz4Caster™, the directions within the template will guide you through preparing your entire Financial Section. If you do not have Biz4Caster™, you can either use the form included in this step or create your own spreadsheet. Whether you are using a pencil and calculator or a sophisticated spreadsheet program, your process will be as follows:

1. Decide which will be your first month in operation and enter the month at the top of each of the twelve columns for your first twelve months of business.

2. Down the left-hand column, enter the name of each unit.

3. In column two, enter your unit price for each of the units entered in the first column.

4. For each unit, forecast the number of units you will sell for each month.

5. For each month, multiply the projected number of units times the unit price.

6. Total the sales dollars forecasted in each column to arrive at the total sales for each month.

7. Total the sales dollars forecasted in each row to arrive at the total sales for each individual unit for your first year.

8. Total all sales across the bottom row or down the right-hand column to arrive at the total sales for your first year.

9. Repeat steps one through eight as necessary, until you have a realistic and achievable sales forecast.

10. Once you are satisfied with your first-year forecast, estimate your growth for Year Two.

11. Once you are satisfied with your second-year forecast, estimate your growth for Year Three.

12. Enter your sales for Years One, Two, and Three into a summary table in your business plan (see the Sales Forecast Summary Example on page 192).

Link: Download a free Sales Forecast Summary Worksheet at **www.riskbuster.com/worksheet/42-sales-forecast-summary**

Tip: Part of the confidence in your Sales Forecast will come from proving portions of your sales. As an example, three line items in my forecast are pre-sold with contracts in place. Back this up with contracts or letters of intent in your Appendices and you are on your way.

Use the following Sales Forecast Worksheet for forecasting your units and dollar amounts for each month in detail for the first 12 months of your business.

Worksheet: Sales Forecast

UNIT NAME	UNIT PRICE	1	2	3	4	5	6	TOTAL
TOTAL SALES								

Link: Download a free Sales Forecast Worksheet from **www.riskbuster.com/worksheet/41-sales-forecast**

Step 55: Explain Your Projections

| MUST HAVE | RECOMMENDED | NICE TO HAVE |

Clarify any points about your projections that might be confusing to the reader.

Example: Explanation of Projections

These financial projections are based on the following assumptions and key points:

1. Year One is from September 1, 2009, to August 31, 2010.

2. E-book sales are expected but not included in these projections, as test marketing is not yet complete.

3. Book and CD projections are based on the assumption that roughly 220 units of each will be sold to Community Futures Development Corporation at distributor rates.

4. Unit 9 projections are based on the assumption that all 24 units will be sold to Community Futures Development Corporation.

5. Unit 12 projections are based on the assumption that the current management contract will continue through the forecasted period.

6. Based on points 3, 4 and 5 above, a total of $66,040 of the Year One revenue is reasonably certain.

7. All unit prices are purposely estimated at conservative rates, while the Cost of Goods Sold calculations are on the high side, making the overall projections very conservative and quite attainable.

Actions

To complete this Element you will need to do the following tasks:

1. As you work through the financial worksheets and tables, keep a list of any points that might be confusing to your reader.

2. By the time you have completed your Financial Elements to draft stage, you should have a healthy list of explanations. If you find it helpful, print a copy of your Financial Elements and study your projections. It can be very effective to have someone read through your projections–their questions may alert you to points that need clarification.

3. Using the Explaining Your Projections Worksheet on the next page, create a list of your assumptions and any notes you believe will help the reader understand how you arrived at your financial calculations.

Link: Download a free Explaining Your Projections Worksheet at **www.riskbuster.com/worksheet/43-explaining-your-projections**

Tip: Take off your rose-colored glasses and create a worst-case financial scenario. Forecast your sales as low as possible, while projecting expenses a little higher than expected. What you want to be able to do is project sales low and expenses high, and still demonstrate that your business will survive (and pay off any loans).

WORKSHEET: EXPLAINING YOUR PROJECTIONS	
Bank Loan–Estimated Interest Rate	
Bank Loan–Estimated Term of Loan	
Owner #1–Monthly Salary	
Owner #2–Monthly Salary	
Percentage of Your Sales That Will Be Paid in Less than 30 Days	
Percentage of Your Sales That Will Be Paid in 30 to 60 Days	
Percentage of Your Sales That Will Be Paid in 60 to 90 Days	
Percentage of Your Sales That Will Be Paid in 90 to 120 Days	
Your WCB Rate Expressed as a Percentage of Payroll	
Your Employer Payroll Burden Expressed as a Percentage of Payroll	
Your Tax Percentage for Year One	
Your Tax Percentage for Year Two	
Your Tax Percentage for Year Three	
The Amount of Your Own Money You Will Put Into Your Business at Start-up	
The Amount of Your Own Non-Cash Equity You Will Put Into Your Business at Start-up	
The Amount of Fixed Assets You Will Put Into Your Business at Start-up	
Your Anticipated Depreciation %	

Step 56: Estimate Your Market Share

MUST HAVE	RECOMMENDED	NICE TO HAVE

Determine your share of the potential sales volume within the market area. A market area and your target market within it will support a certain level of sales of a given product or service. To sell your product or service, you need to understand how the market is divided and what portion you might obtain.

Example: Market Share

	Year One	*Year Two*	*Year Three*
Estimated Number of Customers in Total Market[1]	2,200,000	2,200,000	2,200,000
Average Expenditure Per Customer[2]	$50	$50	$50
Total Potential Market[3]	$110,000,000	$110,000,000	$110,000,000
Total Projected Sales[4]	$128,242	$145,293	$175,725
Market Share[5]	0.11%	0.13%	0.15%

[1]Comes from your Market Research in Steps 16, 18, 19, and 27. Although some growth is expected, have not included growth estimates for Years Two and Three.

[2]Comes from your Market Research and validated by your Customer Survey (Step 27 on page 108).

[3]Comes from multiplying Estimated Number of Customers in Total Market by Average Expenditure per Customer.

[4]Comes from Sales Forecast (Step 54 on page 187).

[5]Comes from dividing Total Projected Sales by Total Potential Market.

Actions

To complete this Element you will need to have completed your primary and secondary market research and your sales forecast, then:

1. Describe how you estimated your market share.

2. Using the summary table below, estimate and enter your total market for Years One, Two, and Three.

3. Determine the average expenditure per customer for Years One, Two, and Three.

4. For each year, multiply the number of customers times the average sale to arrive at the Total Potential Market.

5. Enter your Total Projected Sales for Years One, Two, and Three (from your Sales Forecast).

6. For each year, divide your Total Projected Sales by the Total Potential Market to arrive at your market share percentage.

7. Add any necessary clarifying points to help your reader understand how you arrived at your conclusions.

WORKSHEET: MARKET SHARE			
	Year One	*Year Two*	*Year Three*
Estimated Number of Customers in Total Market			
Average Expenditure Per Customer			
Total Potential Market			
Total Projected Sales			
Market Share			

Link: Download a free Market Share Worksheet from Macrolink at **www.riskbuster.com/worksheet/44-market-share**

Tip: Although the Market Share Element is recommended, it should only be used in conjunction with the bottom-up sales forecast, and ONLY if you can provide reliable estimates for the Total Potential Market. If you are unsure about the Total Potential Market, it is acceptable to eliminate this Element from your business plan.

Step 57: Present Your Cost of Goods Sold

MUST HAVE	RECOMMENDED	NICE TO HAVE

Determine what your products and services will cost and develop your Cost of Goods Sold (COGS) Element.

Example: Cost of Goods Sold

Units	COGS % of Sales	Year One COGS	Year Two COGS
Books-Publisher-Retail	40.00	$5,633	$6,760
Books-Publisher-Bookstores	66.67	3,805	4,566
Books-Publisher-Distributors	80.00	2,048	2,458
Books, Owner–Retail	38.79	7,735	9,282
RiskBuster™ CD–Retail	16.95	795	954
RiskBuster™ CD–Distributors	16.95	900	1,080
Digital Download–Retail	16.95	1,300	1,560
Facilitator Manuals	50.03	700	840
Total COGS		$22,917	$27,500

Note: The preceding table shows 2 years only, due to the limited amount of space available. Your COGS should probably show at least 3 years. As well, I have eliminated all of the rows for Services for which there were no COGS.

Tip: You may ponder whether to show certain costs as COGS or as operating costs in the Cash Flow Forecast. Some costs, such as shipping, might fall either way, depending on how closely tied they are to the product cost. If you can, attach shipping costs directly to each product as a COGS. If not, be sure to include the shipping costs in the Cash Flow in the month during which the expense will be incurred. You have some latitude with this. The main task is to ensure the cost is in one place or the other, not in both.

Actions

To complete this Element you will need to have completed your Sales Forecast and revisit the Pricing and Pricing Strategy Element and the table of costs, prices, mark-ups and COGS percentages. Using your sales projections and the COGS for each unit, then:

1. Work with each unit individually to calculate the COGS for Month One by multiplying the number of units forecasted by the COGS percentage.

2. Repeat task one for each unit for the first twelve months of business.

3. Total the COGS for all units at the bottom of your table.

4. Transfer the total COGS figures to the COGS line in both your Cash Flow Forecast and in your Projected Income Statement.

WORKSHEET: COST OF GOODS SOLD			
Units	COGS % of Sales	Year One COGS	Year Two COGS
1.			
2.			
3.			
4.			
5.			
6.			
7.			
8.			
Total COGS			

Link: Download a free Cost of Goods Sold Worksheet at **www. riskbuster.com/worksheet/45-cost-goods-sold**

Link: Download your free bonus copy of the RiskBuster Business Planner™ at **www.riskbuster.com/RiskBusterBook**

Step 58: Summarize Labor Projections

MUST HAVE	RECOMMENDED	NICE TO HAVE

Estimate what your business will spend on labor for the first twelve months of operation and develop your Labor Projections Element.

Example: Projected Labor Summary

Category	*Year One*	*Year Two*	*Year Three*
Management Salaries	$43,200	$43,200	$43,200
Wages or Subcontractor Fees	7,200	7,200	7,200
Employer Wage Burden	5,040	5,040	5,040
Workers' Compensation	161	161	161
Total Projected Labor	$55,601	$55,601	$55,601

Action

Reach back into the Labor Requirements Worksheet that you calculated in Step 52 (see page 179). If you calculated the time and cost, you need only summarize them for this Element.

You can use the table below in your business plan, or simply show the total labor projection as one line in the cash flow.

WORKSHEET: PROJECTED LABOR SUMMARY			
Category	*Year One*	*Year Two*	*Year Three*
Management Salaries			
Wages or Subcontractor Fees			
Employer Wage Burden			
Workers' Compensation			
Total Projected Labor			

Link: Download a free Projected Labor Summary Worksheet at **www.riskbuster.com/worksheet/46-projected-labor-summary**

Step 59: Develop Your Cash Flow Forecast

MUST HAVE	RECOMMENDED	NICE TO HAVE

Determine the flow of cash into and out of your business. This is the lifeline of your business. It will enable you to clarify how much money you need to operate each month.

The secret to completing a meaningful cash flow is research. The cash flow is an opportunity to build tremendous confidence in your business. That confidence arises from knowing your business and basing your estimates on well-researched assumptions and facts. If you have done your homework, your cash flow will be easy to project.

A solid Cash Flow Forecast will include detailed inflow and outflow of monies from your business for Year One. Year One is typically forecasted in detail, month by month. Years Two and Three are usually projected as a percentage increase over Year One. For example, my business plan projects a 20% increase in sales for the second year and a 30% increase in sales for the third year.

Key points to remember about completing your cash flow:

- Project your sales conservatively.
- Allow more than you think you will need for expenses.
- Cash-in items are entered into a cash flow *during the month they enter your bank account,* and cash-out items are entered *during the month they exit your bank account.*
- Your cash flow is the snapshot you and your banker need in order to determine how much you need for an operating loan.
- Business analysts and bankers will use your cash flow as a measure of whether you know your business.

Example: Cash Flow Forecast

	September	October
Total Sales Forecast	$7,699	$9,147
Cash Receipts (Cash In)		
Cash Sales	6,929	8,232
Accounts Receivable		385
Owner Capital and Non-Cash Equity		
Loan Proceeds	10,850	
Total Cash In	$17,779	$8,617
Cash Disbursements (Cash Out)		
Purchases (Cost of Goods Sold)	1,027	1,533
Advertising	600	600
Auto (Includes R and M, Insurance)	554	554
Interest and Bank Charges	83	83
Insurance/Licenses/Fees	1,700	
Professional (Accounting, Legal)	125	125
Rent (Equipment)		
Rent (Premises)	200	200
Office Supplies and Expenses	200	200
Business Licenses and Permits		
Telephone and Utilities	150	150
Repairs and Maintenance		
Travel and Promotion		400
Management Salaries	3,600	3,600
Wages and Subcontractor Fees	600	600
Employer Wage Burden	420	420
Loan Payments–Principal		418
Loan Payments–Interest		72
Total Cash Out	$9,259	$8,955
Cash Flow Summary		
Opening Balance	0	8,520
Add: Cash In	17,779	8,617
Subtract: Cash Out	9,259	8,955
Closing Cash Balance	$8,520	$8,182

Note: The preceding table shows 2 months only. Your Cash Flow Forecast should be monthly for the first twelve months, followed by a yearly forecast for each of Years Two and Three. If needed, you can forecast as many as 5 years, but keep in mind–the further into the future, the less reliable your forecast will be.

Actions

There are at least a couple of approaches to completing your Cash Flow. One is to do one month or column at a time, from top to bottom. The other is to complete each line item or row from left to right. Use the method that works best for you.

1. At the top of your Cash Flow Worksheet, enter the names of your first 12 months of operation. If you are using the Biz4Caster™, this will already be done for you.

2. From your Sales Forecast, enter all sales in the months during which the cash actually enters your bank account.

3. Enter all other sources of cash entering your bank account during the month they enter your bank account. Include sources of cash other than sales, such as loans or grants.

4. Calculate the Total Cash In amounts for each month and enter the totals into the Total Cash In row.

5. In the Cash Disbursements (Cash Out) section, calculate and enter your total Cost of Goods Sold into each month in the Purchases (Cost of Goods Sold) row.

6. In the Cash Disbursements (Cash Out) section, project your expenses for each of the first 12 months and enter them into the month during which the expense will be paid.

7. Enter your Management Salaries and Wages for each of the first 12 months.

8. Calculate and enter the Employer Wage Burden and Workers' Compensation amounts.

9. Enter any loan payments, usually separating the interest from the principal. This is because the interest is an expense to your business while the principal is not.

10. Calculate the Total Cash Out amounts for each month and enter the totals into the Total Cash Out row.

11. In the Cash Flow Summary, enter zero as your opening balance for the first month.

12. For the first month of operation, enter the Total Cash In and the Total Cash Out.

13. Beginning with the opening balance, add the Total Cash In and then subtract the Total Cash Out. The result is your Closing Cash Balance.

14. Carry the Closing Cash Balance for the first month to become the Opening Balance for the second month.

15. Repeat this process until you have completed all the first 12 months of operation.

16. Calculate the first year's totals for all cash-in and cash-out line items.

17. For Years Two and Three, estimate total amounts for all cash-in and cash-out line items. Most businesses will project a modest increase in sales for Year Two and Year Three, which might necessitate increases for some, but not all expenses.

Link: Download a free Cash Flow Forecast Worksheet from **www. riskbuster.com/worksheet/47-cash-flow-forecast**

Tip: Once you have calculated your expenses, include in your forecast a little extra money for unexpected costs. The higher the risks, the larger you will want your rainy-day fund to be. For most new businesses you will want to add at least 3 to 5%. If it doesn't get used, it becomes profit at the end of the year; if you need it during the year, you will be thankful you included it in your forecasts.

Worksheet: Cash Flow Forecast

	1	2	3	4	5	6
Cash Receipts (Cash In)						
Cash Sales						
Accounts Receivable						
Owner's Capital						
Loan Proceeds						
Total Cash In						
Cash Disbursements (Cash Out)						
Purchases (Cost of Goods Sold)						
Advertising						
Auto (Includes R and M, Insurance)						
Interest and Bank Charges						
Insurance/Licenses/Fees						
Professional (Accounting, Legal)						
Rent (Equipment)						
Rent (Premises)						
Office Supplies and Expenses						
Business Licenses and Permits						
Telephone and Utilities						
Repairs and Maintenance						
Travel and Promotion						
Management Salaries (Drawings)						
Wages and Subcontractor Fees						
Employer Wage Burden						
Loan Payments–Principal						
Loan Payments–Interest						
Total Cash Out						
Cash Flow Summary						
Opening Balance						
Add: Cash In						
Subtract: Cash Out						
Closing Cash Balance						

Note: Although the table above shows a six month cash flow, your cash flow will be monthly for a minimum of twelve months.

Step 60: Identify Your Operating Expenses

MUST HAVE	RECOMMENDED	NICE TO HAVE

Summarize your Operating Expenses for Years One, Two and Three. These are the expenses that will be incurred regardless of whether you make any sales.

Example: Operating Expenses

	Year One	*Year Two*	*Year Three*
Advertising	$7,200	$7,200	$7,200
Auto	6,648	6,648	6,648
Interest and Bank Charges	996	996	996
Insurance/Licenses/Fees	1,700	1,700	1,700
Professional (Accounting, Legal)	1,500	1,500	1,500
Rent (Equipment)			
Rent (Premises)	2,400	2,400	2,400
Office Supplies and Expenses	2,400	2,400	2,400
Business Licenses and Permits	130	130	130
Telephone	1,800	1,800	1,800
Travel and Promotion	4,400	4,400	4,400
Supplies and Small Tools		1,000	1,000
Processing, Legal, Broker Fees	850	850	850
Auto (Gas, Oil)	3,000	3,000	3,000
Management Salaries	43,200	43,200	43,200
Wages and Subcontractor Fees	7,200	7,200	7,200
Employer Wage Burden	5,040	5,040	5,040
Workers' Compensation	161	161	161
Loan Payments–Interest	639	285	3
Total Operating Expenses	$89,264	$89,910	$89,629

Actions

To complete this step you will first need to complete your Cash Flow Forecast, then:

1. Enter the totals for all three years into the following table.

2. Check each expense thoroughly to make sure it is accurate and neither over nor underestimated.

3. If changes are needed, go back to the Cash Flow Worksheet and enter them there.

Note: If you have completed the Cash Flow Forecast (see Step 59 on page 199), you already have the Operating Expenses for all three years.

WORKSHEET: OPERATING EXPENSES			
	Year One	*Year Two*	*Year Three*
Advertising			
Auto			
Interest and Bank Charges			
Insurance/Licenses/Fees			
Professional (Accounting, Legal)			
Rent (Equipment)			
Rent (Premises)			
Office Supplies and Expenses			
Business Licenses and Permits			
Telephone and Utilities			
Repairs and Maintenance			
Management Salaries			
Wages and Subcontractor Fees			
Employer Wage Burden			
Loan Payments - Interest			
Total Operating Expenses			

Link: Download a free Operating Expenses Worksheet from **www. riskbuster.com/worksheet/48-operating-expenses**

Step 61: Develop Your Projected Income Statement

MUST HAVE	RECOMMENDED	NICE TO HAVE

Determine your profit or loss for each of the first three years.

The Income Statement, also referred to as the Profit and Loss Statement, tells you whether your business is earning profits or losing money. Do not confuse this with the financial view presented in the Cash Flow Forecast, which tells you how much money is remaining in your bank account at the beginning and end of each month. Contrary to what is believed by many new business owners, the Cash Flow Forecast does not tell how much a business is earning. I recommend that you re-read this paragraph until you understand it–it's important.

The formula for the income statement is:

Sales – Cost of Goods Sold = Gross Margin

Gross Margin – Total Operating Expenses – Depreciation = Net Income (Or Loss) Before Tax

---

Link: Download your free bonus copy of the RiskBuster Business Planner™ at **www.riskbuster.com/RiskBusterBook**

Tip: If you plan to take a salary or owner's drawings, I recommend that you project the amounts monthly for the first year in business and annually for Year Two and 3. Projecting the drawings when they *actually come out of your bank account* will do two important things for your business plan:
- It will make your cash flow projection more accurate, and
- It will enable the reader of your business plan to see how much money you plan to extract from your business.

Example: Projected Income Statement

	Year One	Year Two	Year Three
Sales Forecast	$128,242	$145,293	$175,725
Minus: Cost of Goods Sold	22,917	27,500	35,750
Gross Profit Margin	105,326	117,793	139,975
Gross Profit Margin Percentage	82.13%	81.07%	79.66%
Other Cash Received (Grants)	0.00	0.00	0.00
Operating Expenses			
Advertising	7,200	7,200	7,200
Auto	6,648	6,648	6,648
Interest and Bank Charges	996	996	996
Insurance/Licenses/Fees	1,700	1,700	1,700
Professional (Accounting, Legal)	1,500	1,500	1,500
Rent (Premises)	2,400	2,400	2,400
Office Supplies and Expenses	2,400	2,400	2,400
Business Licenses and Permits	130	130	130
Telephone	1,800	1,800	1,800
Utilities			
Repairs and Maintenance			
Travel and Promotion	4,400	4,400	4,400
Processing, Legal, Broker Fees	850	850	850
Auto (Gas, Oil)	3,000	3,000	3,000
Management Salaries	43,200	43,200	43,200
Wages and Subcontractor Fees	7,200	7,200	7,200
Employer Wage Burden	5,040	5,040	5,040
Workers' Compensation	161	161	161
Interest on Long-Term Debt	639	285	3
Supplies and Small Tools	0	1,000	1,000
Total Operating Expenses	$89,264	$89,910	$89,629
Summary			
Gross Profit and Other Income	105,326	117,793	139,975
Total Operating Expenses	89,264	89,910	89,629
Subtract: Depreciation	4,000	4,800	5,600
Net Income Before Tax	12,061	23,083	44,746
Income Tax	2,125	4,067	7,884
Net Income After Tax	$9,936	$19,015	$36,862

Example: Projected Income Summary

	Year One	Year Two	Year Three
Sales Forecast	$128,242	$145,293	$175,725
Minus Cost of Goods Sold	22,917	27,500	35,750
Equals Gross Profit Margin	105,326	117,793	139,975
Subtract Total Operating Expenses	89,264	89,910	89,629
Subtract Depreciation	4,000	4,800	5,600
Equals Net Income Before Tax	$12,061	$23,083	$44,746

Actions

If you are using Biz4Caster™, your Income Statement will be done automatically.

To complete this Element, you will first need to complete the Elements called Sales Forecast, Labor Projections, and Cash Flow Forecast, then:

1. If you use the Income Statement Worksheet, this process still applies, except that you will need to complete your calculations manually.

2. Enter the total Revenue or Sales for Year One.

3. Enter the total Cost of Goods Sold (COGS) for Year One.

4. Calculate the Gross Profit Margin by subtracting COGS from Revenue or Sales and enter the amount in the Summary.

5. Enter all Operating Expenses for Year One. (These amounts will come from the totals column in the Cash Flow Forecast.)

6. Total the Operating Expenses column and enter the amount in the Summary.

7. Calculate Depreciation for Year One for all equipment over $250 in value. This may require that you use a separate Worksheet. Enter the total amount.

8. In the Summary, use this formula to calculate the Net Income: Gross Profit Margin minus Total Operating Expenses plus Depreciation equals Net Income Before Tax.

9. Determine what percentage your sales will increase for Years Two and Three, and repeat the process above, with careful consideration to any potential changes to each cost.

WORKSHEET: PROJECTED INCOME SUMMARY			
	Year One	*Year Two*	*Year Three*
Sales Forecast			
Minus Cost of Goods Sold			
Equals Gross Profit Margin			
Subtract Total Operating Expenses			
Subtract Depreciation			
Equals Net Income Before Tax			

Link: Download a free Projected Income Statement Worksheet **www.riskbuster.com/worksheet/49-projected-income-statement**

Link: Download a free Projected Income Summary Worksheet at **www.riskbuster.com/worksheet/50-projected-income-summary**

Tip: There is no benefit to using all three tables (Operating Expense Summary, Projected Income Statement and Projected Income Summary) in your business plan. If you use the Projected Income Statement, you can dispense with the other two tables. If you include the two Summary tables, there's no point to including the Projected Income Statement.

Worksheet: Projected Income Statement

	Year One	*Year Two*	*Year Three*
Sales Forecast			
Minus: Cost of Goods Sold			
Gross Profit Margin			
Gross Profit Margin Percentage			
Other Cash Received (Grants)			
Operating Expenses			
Advertising			
Auto			
Interest and Bank Charges			
Insurance/Licenses/Fees			
Professional (Accounting, Legal)			
Rent (Equipment)			
Rent (Premises)			
Office Supplies and Expenses			
Business Licenses and Permits			
Telephone			
Utilities			
Repairs and Maintenance			
Travel and Promotion			
Processing, Legal, Broker Fees			
Auto (Gas, Oil)			
Management Salaries			
Wages and Subcontractor Fees			
Employer Wage Burden			
Workers' Compensation			
Interest on Long-Term Debt			
Supplies and Small Tools			
Total Operating Expenses			
Summary			
Gross Profit and Other Income			
Total Operating Expenses			
Subtract: Depreciation			
Net Income Before Tax			
Income Tax			
Net Income After Tax			

Step 62: Determine Your Break-Even

MUST HAVE	RECOMMENDED	NICE TO HAVE

Determine the point in the year when your business will break even or begin to earn profit from sales.

Example: Break-Even Analysis

	Year One	*Year Two*	*Year Three*
Total Sales	$128,242	$145,293	$175,725
Total Cost of Goods Sold	22,917	27,500	35,750
Equals: Gross Profit Margin	105,326	117,793	139,975
Gross Profit Margin %	82.13%	81.07%	79.66%
Total Operating Expenses	89,264	89,910	89,629
Break-Even Point	$112,181	$117,410	$125,379

Actions

To complete this Element, you will need to have completed the first version of all or most of the other Financial Elements to enable you to calculate different scenarios, then:

1. Calculate your Total Sales for Year One.

2. Calculate your Total Cost of Goods Sold for Year One.

3. Calculate your Total Gross Margin for Year One (#1 Minus #2).

4. Calculate your Gross Margin Percentage for Year One (#3 Divided by #1).

5. Calculate your Total Operating Expenses for Year One.

6. Determine your Break-Even Point for Year One (#2 Plus #5).

7. Repeat the above steps 1 through 6 for Years Two and Year Three.

WORKSHEET: BREAK-EVEN ANALYSIS			
	Year One	*Year Two*	*Year Three*
Total Sales			
Total Cost of Goods Sold			
Equals: Gross Profit Margin			
Gross Profit Margin %			
Total Operating Expenses			
Break-Even Point			

Note: This method of calculating break-even will be accurate for the product or service mix you have forecasted for any particular scenario. If you sell more or less of any given unit, the ratios can change, which may also change the break-even point.

Link: Download a free Break Even Analysis Worksheet at **www. riskbuster.com/worksheet/51-break-even-analysis**

Tip: When seeking to borrow money to start your business, be conservative but realistic. Be sure to ask for enough money to succeed in your efforts.

Step 63: Build a Pro Forma Balance Sheet

MUST HAVE	RECOMMENDED	NICE TO HAVE

Determine the net worth of your business. It is a snapshot of your business at a specific time. If it is developed for some point in the future, it is referred to as a Pro Forma Balance Sheet.

When doing this Element, it is important to keep in mind that you are forecasting, not accounting; therefore, you are estimating.

Actions

1. To determine the net worth of your business, subtract liabilities from assets. The equation for this is: assets minus liabilities equal net worth.

2. Estimate your total current assets. This will include all cash, inventory, prepaid expenses, and accounts receivable.

3. Estimate your total fixed assets. This might include investments and capital equipment.

4. Determine the current liabilities. This might include financial obligations, taxes owed, accounts payable, and unpaid bills.

5. Calculate your long-term liabilities such as mortgages, bank loans and equipment leases.

Subtract your total liabilities from your total assets to determine your net worth. Net worth is the equity or money you have invested in your business. A Pro Forma Balance Sheet Example and a Worksheet are on the following two pages.

Link: Download a free Pro Forma Balance Sheet Worksheet at **www. riskbuster.com/worksheet/52-pro-forma-balance-sheet**

Example: Pro Forma Balance Sheet

ASSETS	Start	Year One	Year Two	Year Three
CURRENT ASSETS				
Cash and Bank Accounts	$10,850	$22,209	$35,961	$75,336
Accounts Receivable		1,932	2,188	2,647
Inventory				
Prepaid Rent				
TTL CURRENT ASSETS	10,850	24,140	38,150	77,983
FIXED AND OTHER ASSETS				
Fixed Assets	20,000	20,000	24,000	28,000
Other Assets				
Accumulated Depreciation		(4,000)	(8,800)	(14,400)
TTL FIXED/OTHER ASSETS	20,000	16,000	15,200	13,600
TOTAL ASSETS	30,850	40,140	53,350	91,583
LIABILITIES				
CURRENT LIABILITIES				
Accounts Payable		1,988	1,844	1,885
Corporate Income Tax Payable		2,125	4,067	7,884
Current Part Long-Term Debt		5,604	487	
TTL CURRENT LIABILITIES		9,717	6,399	9,770
LONG-TERM DEBT				
Mortgages and Liens Payable	10,850	487		
Shareholder's Loan	20,000	20,000	18,000	16,000
TOTAL LONG-TERM DEBT	30,850	20,487	18,000	16,000
TOTAL LIABILITIES	30,850	30,204	24,399	25,770
OWNERS' EQUITY				
Retained Earnings		9,936	28,951	65,813
TOTAL EQUITY & LIABILITIES	$30,850	$40,140	$53,350	$91,583

	Start	Year One	Year Two	Year Three
ASSETS				
CURRENT ASSETS				
Cash and Bank Accounts				
Accounts Receivable				
Inventory				
Prepaid Rent				
TTL CURRENT ASSETS				
FIXED AND OTHER ASSETS				
Fixed Assets				
Other Assets				
Accumulated Depreciation				
TTL FIXED/OTHER ASSETS				
TOTAL ASSETS				
LIABILITIES				
CURRENT LIABILITIES				
Accounts Payable				
Corporate Income Tax Payable				
Current Part Long-Term Debt				
TTL CURRENT LIABILITIES				
LONG-TERM DEBT				
Mortgages and Liens Payable				
Shareholder's Loan				
TTL LONG-TERM DEBT				
TOTAL LIABILITIES				
OWNERS' EQUITY				
Retained Earnings				
TOTAL EQUITY & LIABILITIES				

Step 64: Identify Your Start-Up Expenses

MUST HAVE	RECOMMENDED	NICE TO HAVE

Determine your Start-up Expenses. These are all the costs related to getting your business up and running. It's important to understand that you have some discretion as to which costs get included in start-up. Some analysts will include all the costs for months prior to the opening day and reflect this in the business plan by including a 15-month rather than a 12-month cash flow projection. I prefer to use a 12-month cash flow projection with the start-up costs slotted into the first month.

Another issue that can generate confusion is the difference between a start-up loan, an operating loan, a capital equipment loan, and an inventory loan. You do not need to get tangled up with the labels, as your banker or lending agency will slot the amounts into the appropriate categories.

Practically speaking, you need enough money at start-up to get you successfully to the operating stage.

Example: Start-Up Expenses

	Have	*Need*	*Totals*
Start-up Inventory		$1,500	$1,500
Advertising	800		800
Auto	554		554
Interest and Bank Charges	83		83
Insurance/Licenses/Fees	1,700		1,700
Office Supplies and Expenses	200		200
Business Licenses and Permits	130		130
Telephone	150		150
Owner's Equity, Fixed Assets	20,000		20,000
Purchase of Other Assets	0		
Processing, Legal, Broker Fees	850		850
Auto (Gas, Oil)	250		250
Management Salaries	3,600		3,600
Wages and Subcontractor Fees	600		600
Employer Wage Burden	420		420
Workers' Compensation	13		13
Total Start-up Expenses	29,350	$1,500	$30,850

Actions

To complete this Element, you will need to determine what you must have in place to begin conducting business, and you must have researched the related costs, then:

1. Enter all amounts you will need in place to begin doing business.

2. In listing your Start-up Expenses, note that the Cash Flow Forecast includes all costs for the twelve months following the start-up. Be sure that you do *not* duplicate expenses by including them in both start-up and in your Operating Expenses.

The Worksheet on the following page can be used to develop your Start-up Expenses Element. Work with your banker or business analyst to determine the best package for your situation.

Tip: Include the equity you bring to the business in your start-up calculations. For example, if you own tools and equipment that you will roll into the business, show the value of the items as owner equity at start-up. This will strengthen your business proposal. If you include any equipment, such as a vehicle, with loans outstanding, be sure to include both the asset and the liability (your equity and the amount owing on the loan).

Tip: Project the Owner's Drawings conservatively. Unless your business can truly sustain higher Owner's Drawings, keep them low. If you are planning to borrow money or access a government grant, paying yourself a conservative rate shows diligence and commitment.

WORKSHEET: START-UP EXPENSES			
Start-Up Expenses	*Have*	*Need*	*Totals*
Start-up Inventory			
Advertising			
Auto			
Interest and Bank Charges			
Insurance/Licenses/Fees			
Professional (Accounting, Legal)			
Rent (Equipment)			
Rent (Premises)			
Office Supplies and Expenses			
Business Licenses and Permits			
Telephone			
Utilities			
Repairs and Maintenance			
Travel and Promotion			
Purchase Fixed Assets			
Purchase Other Assets			
Processing, Legal, Broker Fees			
Auto (Gas, Oil)			
Management Salaries			
Wages and Subcontractor Fees			
Employer Wage Burden			
Workers' Compensation			
Loan Payments–Interest			
Total Start-up Expenses			

Link: Download a free Start-up Expenses Worksheet from **www. riskbuster.com/worksheet/53-start-expenses**

Step 65: Clarify Sources and Uses of Funds

MUST HAVE	RECOMMENDED	NICE TO HAVE

List all sources and uses of funds at start-up. This Element is very much tied to the Start-up Expenses Element, in that your use of funds is a summary of the Start-up Expenses.

Example: Use and Source of Funds

Use of Funds		Source of Funds	
Operating Expenses	Amount	Owner Investment	Amount
Start-up Expenses	$10,850	Owner Cash	$10,000
Other Operating Exp.		Owner Equity	10,000
Owner Equip. Equity	10,000	Debt Sources	
Other		Family	
		Friends	10,850
Capital Purchases		Community Futures	
		Chartered Banks	
Purchase Fixed Assets	10,000	Credit Union	
Purchase Other Assets		Angel	
Total Funding Use	$30,850	Total Funding Source	$30,850

Tip: With the exception of unusual circumstances, you must come to the table with equity—the more equity, the stronger your proposal. Unless you're dealing with a development lender or have access to a strong co-signer, the owner must have a minimum of 10% equity or investment in a loan package, but 20% investment by the owner makes a stronger case. Research your target lender to determine his or her requirements.

Actions

To complete this Element, you will need to have completed the Start-up Expense calculations, then:

1. Working from the Start-up Expenses table, calculate and enter the dollar amounts in the appropriate cells in the following table for uses (what the money will pay for) and for sources (where the money will come from).

2. This Element will help you clarify whether you need financing and how much you need.

3. The table communicates to the reader how much you are investing and how much you are requesting from other sources.

4. The totals at the bottom of the sources column must equal the total at the bottom of the uses column.

WORKSHEET: USE AND SOURCE OF FUNDS			
Use of Funds		*Source of Funds*	
Operating Expenses	**Amount**	**Owner Investment**	**Amount**
Start-up Expenses		Owner Cash	
Other Operating Exp.		Owner Equity	
Owner Equip. Equity		**Debt Sources**	
Other		Family	
		Friends	
Capital Purchases		Community Futures	
		Chartered Banks	
Purchase Fixed Assets		Credit Union	
Purchase Other Assets		Angel	
Total Needed		Total Sourced	

Link: Download a free Use and Source of Funds Worksheet at **www.riskbuster.com/worksheet/54-use-and-source-funds**

Assemble Your Appendices

The purpose of this Section is to provide all additional information that supports the objectives of the plan. The contents of this Section will vary according to the requirements of the lender or investor. I recommend that you prepare the Elements of this Section for your own benefit and that they be provided with the business plan as required by the target audience or readers.

On the following page is an example of an Appendices Goal Worksheet for Macrolink Action Plans Inc. The list includes most of the common Appendices or supporting documents for many small businesses. The goal of this exercise is to eliminate the unnecessary ones, but don't hesitate to add any others you deem to be important for your plan.

Action

You have already dealt with setting up your Appendices files and folders in Step 11 (see page 65). To avoid duplicating your efforts, go back and review what you did then.

Identify what you need to do to for each of the Appendices you have chosen to use.

Tip: The 24 Appendices, Steps 66 to 89 (see pages 224 to 259), may be much less work than you envision. Here's why:
1. By the time you eliminate the irrelevant and unnecessary Appendices, your efforts will be very focused on a few important Elements.
2. The number of Appendices needed will depend on the intended use of your business plan. If you're using it to apply for a loan or to attract investors, you will need a full complement of supporting information and a high degree of proof. If your plan is simply for your own use, you may choose not to include any Appendices.
3. Some Appendices, such as your resume, will probably already be done and perhaps only need to be updated. Others you will have gathered while completing your market research.

Example: Appendices Goal

Appendices Element	Need to Do
1. Resumés	Update
2. Personal Net Worth Statement(s)	Use Bank form
3. Certificates and Accreditation	Not Applicable
4. Historical Financial Statements	3-year summary
5. Organizational Charts	Not Applicable
6. Board or Band Council Resolution	Not Applicable
7. List of References	Include a brief list
8. Letters of Reference	Include testimonials
9. Letters of Intent	Not Applicable
10. Contracts or Offers	Available on request
11. Partnership Agreement	Not Applicable
12. Lease Agreement	Not Applicable
13. Insurance Documents	Not Applicable
14. Price Lists	Not Applicable
15. Price Quotes	Not Applicable
16. Appraisals	Not Applicable
17. Market Survey Results	Will provide on request
18. Map of Area	Not Applicable
19. Environmental Information	Not Applicable
20. Publicity	Am collecting
21. Promotional Material	After start-up
22. Product Literature	One-page descriptions
23. Technical Specifications	Not Applicable
24. Glossary of Terms	Not Applicable

Appendices Element	Need to Do
1. Resumés	
2. Personal Net Worth Statement(s)	
3. Certificates and Accreditation	
4. Historical Financial Statements	
5. Organizational Charts	
6. Board or Band Council Resolution	
7. List of References	
8. Letters of Reference	
9. Letters of Intent	
10. Contracts or Offers	
11. Partnership Agreement	
12. Lease Agreement	
13. Insurance Documents	
14. Price Lists	
15. Price Quotes	
16. Appraisals	
17. Market Survey Results	
18. Map of Area	
19. Environmental Information	
20. Publicity	
21. Promotional Material	
22. Product Literature	
23. Technical Specifications	
24. Glossary of Terms	

Link: Download a free Appendices Goals Worksheet from **www.riskbuster.com/worksheet/55-appendices-goals**

Step 66: Build a Resumé

MUST HAVE	RECOMMENDED	NICE TO HAVE

Create a resumé that demonstrates why you are qualified to operate your business.

A resumé is a concise inventory of your personal experiences, your educational background, and any job-related personal traits. Job seekers prepare resumés to submit to prospective employers, while entrepreneurs use their resumé to support their business plan and proposals. Your resumé outlines what you personally offer to make your business successful. A strong resumé helps you make a good impression and in some cases is the only means of securing a loan or a client, so prepare it carefully.

In making their decisions, lenders and investors place the highest importance on the quality of the manager or management team. A poorly written resumé can detract from an otherwise excellent business plan.

Taking the time to prepare a professional looking resumé will give you a definite edge over your competitors. It indicates a businesslike approach and shows motivation and initiative.

Tip: Choose the resumé style that will present your experience in the best possible way.

Tip: Your resumé must be accurate. Poor grammar and misspelled words will erode the credibility you are working so hard to build.

Action Words and Strong Descriptors

Consider the following words when preparing your resumé or completing your application. They will help you make a positive, favorable impression on the reader.

ACTION WORDS CHECKLIST		
☐ Accomplished	☐ Directed	☐ Maintained
☐ Achieved	☐ Employed	☐ Managed
☐ Administered	☐ Engineered	☐ Organized
☐ Analyzed	☐ Equipped	☐ Participated
☐ Built	☐ Established	☐ Processed
☐ Communicated	☐ Expanded	☐ Repaired
☐ Completed	☐ Guided	☐ Sold
☐ Controlled	☐ Implemented	☐ Specialized
☐ Coordinated	☐ Improved	☐ Supervised
☐ Created	☐ Initiated	☐ Trained
☐ Designed	☐ Investigated	☐ Worked
☐ Developed	☐ Led	
STRONG DESCRIPTORS CHECKLIST		
☐ Capable	☐ Knowledgeable	☐ Resourceful
☐ Competent	☐ Positive	☐ Stable
☐ Consistent	☐ Productive	☐ Successful
☐ Effective	☐ Proficient	☐ Varied background
☐ Efficient	☐ Profitable	☐ Versatile
☐ Experienced	☐ Qualified	☐ Well educated

Tip: Spacing is important in creating an impression of neatness and orderliness. It is better to reduce the amount of information on the page than to crowd it with too many details. When you glance at your finished copy, it should look neat, clean, and easy to read. Limit your resumé to one or two pages.

Parts of a Combination Resumé

Personal Information • Name and contact information
Objective • Tells the employers the position you want
Key Strengths • Points of primary interest to the employer
Accomplishments • Summarizes areas of expertise with brief facts
Work History • In reverse chronological order–Dates, Job Title, Name of Business, Skills and Accomplishments, Duties
Education • Shows training related to the position • Put this section near the top if it is more important to the employer
Interests • Optional–Fitness, Community Involvement, Volunteer Work
References • Option–have separate reference sheet or note on the resumé that references are available upon request • Use only references that are current and confirmed • Ensure that the contact information for each reference is accurate

WORKSHEET: RESUMÉ
Personal Information
Objective
Key Strengths
Accomplishments
Work History
Education
Interests
References

Actions

This task list can be carried out using a pencil and the Resumé Worksheet for Entrepreneurs in the Appendices, or by loading the information directly into your word processing program.

1. Gather and organize your personal and business contact information, such as your name, address, telephone numbers, fax number, email address, and website address.

2. List and prioritize your key strengths according to their importance to the person or team who will receive your resumé. Use the list of positive words in the Action Words and Strong Descriptors checklists (see page 225) to help you arrive at a dynamic list of key strengths that sell you, but don't overdo it.

3. Compile a list of your accomplishments. This is optional, as you may choose to simply list your accomplishments under each segment of your work history. Once you have listed your achievements, prioritize them according to their importance to the reader of your resumé or business plan.

4. List your past jobs or business experiences, beginning with the most recent and working your way backwards in time. For each listing, include dates or number of years of the engagement, your job title, name of the organization, and a list of the most relevant skills, accomplishments, and duties. You can pick and choose the parts of your work history that are most relevant to the reader of your resumé.

5. List your educational and training achievements, beginning with the most recent and working your way back in time. If this segment is more important to the reader of your resumé, feel free to place it before the work history.

6. Briefly list your interests. Your objective with this is to reflect that you have a life, but not so much of a life that you're too busy to work. Use this segment to reflect aspects of your life or personality that are not obvious in other parts of your resumé. For example, fitness, community involvement, volunteering, hobbies, etc. This segment is optional.

7. Compile a list of references and either include them at the end of your resumé or state that references are available upon request. In all cases, be sure to ask permission of anyone you intend to use as a reference, and ensure that you provide accurate, up-to-date contact information for all references.

Link: Download a free Resumé for Entrepreneurs Worksheet at **www.riskbuster.com/worksheet/40-operational-action-plan**

Tip: If you are unable to fit your resumé on two full pages, you might be including too much detail or getting too wordy. Keep sifting until you are able to fit the required information on two pages or less while still maintaining adequate white space. The amount of time you invest in building a succinct document will be appreciated by the reader. Many professionals with hiring responsibilities simply toss longer resumés in the brown file, never to be read.

Tip: If you have already developed the Owner Element, review it to be sure it is consistent with your resumé.

Tip: Give careful consideration as to whether to include both the Owner Element and your resumé. If only one is necessary for your business plan, include only the one that will better serve your purpose.

Step 67: Determine Personal Net Worth

MUST HAVE	RECOMMENDED	NICE TO HAVE

Provide a potential lender with a clear snapshot of your current financial situation. You want to provide enough information for the lender to make an informed decision as to whether to invest in your business venture.

Action

Determine whether you need a Personal Net Worth Statement. If one is required, gather the information, complete the form and attach it to your loan application or business plan. If you are applying for a loan, the lender will probably have a preferred format for you to use.

Tip: Do not inflate the value of your assets. Inflating the value of assets above what they are really worth tends to deflate your credibility with your reader. If you are seeking to borrow money, your task is to build credibility with the lending agency. Consider having a third party provide a valuation of certain assets, real estate, equipment, etc.

Tip: Your personal net worth tells a story about how you manage money in your personal life. It is also a reasonably accurate reflection of how you will manage money in your business. Use this Worksheet to identify any financial issues you can tidy up before approaching a lending agency. For example, can you consolidate debts or sell any toys (boats, campers, bikes, motorized water or winter machines) to reduce or eliminate unnecessary debt?

Step 68: Include Certificates and Accreditation

MUST HAVE	RECOMMENDED	NICE TO HAVE

Provide any certificates and accreditation that will build your credibility as owner and manager of your proposed business.

Provide only the certificates that are relevant to this business. Do not overdo it. Your purpose here is to build your credibility, not pass a paperweight test.

Here are some points to consider in gathering documents for this Element:

- Is the document relevant to this business?
- Is the achievement related to the type of work you will do in the business?
- Is the certificate from a recognized institution?
- How credible is the organization to the reader(s) of your business plan?
- Is the document clean and professional looking?
- Does the document add credibility to your business plan?

Link: Download a free List of Certificates and Documents Worksheet from **www.riskbuster.com/worksheet/57-list-certificates-and-documents**

Tip: If you have quite a few documents for this Element, consider scanning or copying them at a reduced size in order to get more than one per page. A small investment in this may provide you with an efficient and professional tool to be reused many times in the future.

Step 69: Provide Historical Financials

MUST HAVE	RECOMMENDED	NICE TO HAVE

Provide historical financial statements for existing businesses. This step is applicable only for those aspiring to buy or grow an existing business.

If You're Buying a Business

When purchasing an existing business, historical financial statements are critical. You will want them first for yourself, to clarify what you are buying and validate the seller's claims of vast profits and no problems forever. If you are planning to borrow money to complete the purchase, your lender will not even begin the dialogue without financial statements for the past three years of operation.

Tip: When buying a business, if the seller offers any resistance to providing you with historical financial statements, you should probably not pursue the deal any further. Unless the business is less than three years old, you can expect to see the past three years' historical financial statements, including income statements and balance sheets for all three years.

Tip: When the seller provides you with historical financial statements, it is entirely reasonable to require you to sign a confidentiality or non-disclosure agreement. Be sure the agreement permits you to share the information with your accountant, lawyer, and potential bankers or lenders.

Step 70: Create Organizational Charts

MUST HAVE	RECOMMENDED	NICE TO HAVE

Make it easy for your reader to understand how the human resource part of your business is organized.

If you are a single owner-operator, you need not build an organizational chart unless you have several personalities with complex lines of reporting to each other!

Here is a sample organizational chart:

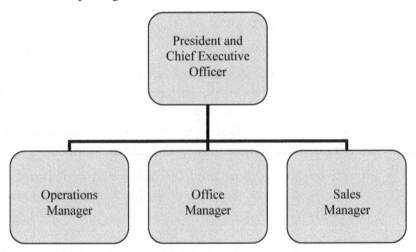

Step 71: Get the Approval of Your Board

MUST HAVE	RECOMMENDED	NICE TO HAVE

Provide documentation to prove that your business plan is supported by the legal decision makers for the organization.

You may require this type of documentation if your business:

- Is a not-for-profit or government-owned organization.
- Requires the support of a political body such as a First Nations government.
- Has a Board of Directors.
- Is a publicly held corporation.
- No example is provided here because each Board of Directors will use a standard format for such purposes. For example, First Nations will usually use a Band Council Resolution (BCR), whereas a Board of Directors for a non-profit organization might provide a copy of the approved Board motion.
- If you do not serve or need the permission of a Board of Directors, skip this step and drop this Element from your Appendices.

Tip: If you must get the permission of a Board of Directors for your business idea, you may have to complete your business plan first. Your business plan then becomes the communication tool you use to get the permission of the Board.

Step 72: Build Your List of References

MUST HAVE	RECOMMENDED	NICE TO HAVE

Provide your reader with a clear path to research you and your business plan: Communicate with key references.

Here are some tips on building a list of references:

- Call them and ask permission to use their name.

- Confirm that you have accurate contact information for each reference.

- Never share contact information unless your reference has specifically given you permission to do so.

- Cut any negative, dated, or uncertain references from your list.

- Use only the references most relevant to your reader.

Example: List of References

Name, Title	Business	Location	Phone	Email
Donna Wood, President	Wood Delivery, Inc.	Rock Creek	357-1179	donna@wd.ca

WORKSHEET: LIST OF REFERENCES				
Name, Title	Business	Location	Phone	Email

Link: Download a free List of References Worksheet from **www. riskbuster.com/worksheet/58-list-references**

Tip: Be sure to obtain current permission from your references. A valued reference that has time to prepare is more inclined to think of nice things to say about you. A surprised reference is not always your best reference!

Step 73: Include Letters of Reference

MUST HAVE	RECOMMENDED	NICE TO HAVE

The challenge with letters of reference is that they quickly become outdated. Nonetheless, a glowing letter of reference is a strong marketing tool to help support your business plan.

Unfortunately you will not have a lot of control over the quality of reference letters, which will be mostly determined by the skill level of the writer. It is inappropriate to provide a sample or to suggest what should go into a reference letter, unless specifically requested by the person you approach. In most cases, a savvy ex-boss will ask what the reference letter will be used for. This creates an opening for you to explain the purpose of the letter and mention the important attributes the recipient might be looking for in your application. Here are some things to keep in mind about letters of reference:

- The appearance of the letter is important. The letter will be more credible if it is typewritten and on the writer's letterhead.

- The letter should include a date and be current.

- The letter should include reference to your relationship with the writer. For example, was he or she your supervisor, accountant, or contract manager? If this information is not included in the reference, ensure that you provide it some other way.

- Your reference letters will be stronger if they come from an individual or organization the reader can relate to. If you are submitting your business plan for the purpose of obtaining a loan, your strongest reference letters might be from current customers and trade accounts where you have a track record for paying your bills on time.

Example: Letter of Reference

Macrolink Action Plans Inc.
Box 101, Prince George, BC V2L 4R9

January 3, 2009

To Whom It May Concern:

I have known Theresa Williams since the early 1990s, where she contracted on a few occasions with my business to provide safety-related workshops to our clients.

Theresa's responsibilities included traveling to remote locations; setting up facilities at the client's location; greeting participants as they arrived; and providing the training. She was also responsible for all administrative duties, including reporting, grading participant's exams, and summarizing workshop evaluations.

Theresa has shown the kind of initiative that is necessary to be successful in the training business. She has excellent organizational and presentation skills and is clearly focused on the needs of the client. She is a self-starter and a conscientious worker, and she has an excellent work ethic.

I recommend Theresa to you as a competent trainer and facilitator. If you have any further questions, please feel free to call me at 250-612-1234.

Sincerely,

Dan Boudreau
President and CEO

Step 74: Include Letters of Intent

MUST HAVE	RECOMMENDED	NICE TO HAVE

Letters of intent are statements written by individuals or organizations declaring their intention to commit to something, typically to use or purchase a product or service, but also for other things.

A Letter of Intent can be appropriate for situations where you are not able to sign a contract. It can add valuable strength and credibility to your claims in the business plan. For example, you might build a sales forecast on the assumption that key clients will make regular purchases, even though no contract exists; a clear Letter of Intent from one or more key clients or customers will help you build your business case.

Unlike a letter of reference, it is okay to provide a template or suggested wording for the writer of your Letter of Intent. The people you approach will be busy, and unless they have written letters of intent before, they are unlikely to know exactly what you are looking for. I suggest you put together a generic Letter of Intent to provide to those who commit to doing one for you.

An effective Letter of Intent:

- Must include the date it was written, and it should be current, written on letterhead, and signed.

- Must come from a credible decision maker or person with the authority to honor promises made in the letter.

- Will be stronger if more specific, weaker if more general. In other words, it will help your business case if the writer states he or she will purchase an amount of goods or services within a specific time period. A general or vaguely written Letter of Intent doesn't provide a banker with a strong foundation on which to base a decision.

Example: Letter of Intent

ABC Business Development Centre
Box 1000, Prince George, BC V2L 4J3

January 3, 2009

To Whom It May Concern:

The purpose of this letter is to express our intention to purchase products and services from Macrolink Action Plans Inc.

In the 12 months beginning September 2009, I will contract the services of Mr. Boudreau for a minimum of 5 days each month at a rate of $495 per day.

If you have any questions, please call me at 250-612-1234.

Sincerely,

John Williams
Executive Director

Step 75: Include Signed Contracts and Offers

MUST HAVE	RECOMMENDED	NICE TO HAVE

There is nothing quite as strong as a signed contract to substantiate your assumption or claim that a customer will buy your product or service. A written offer is almost as strong in terms of credibility, certainly as strong as a contract.

No example is provided here because the nature and type of contracts varies so widely. The important thing is that you research your particular Industry and get to know what the Industry standard is for contracts for your business.

If you are bidding or responding to calls for proposals for government or Industry contracts, the buyer will usually dictate and provide the contract. Most government agencies work from boilerplate contract templates that they adapt to your specific situation. In these instances, your only real control lies with how you write your proposal and how thoroughly you read the contract before signing it.

If you are not experienced at writing and reading contracts, I strongly recommend that you engage a competent lawyer to assist you. In spite of all those bad lawyer jokes, a good lawyer will save you money.

Tip: If your contract is too lengthy to include, consider including only the pertinent pages from the contract. This might be the first or Cover Page, signature page, and possibly specific financial or deliverables pages. If you choose this path, be sure to state that the full document(s) are available upon request.

Step 76: Create a Partnership Agreement

MUST HAVE	RECOMMENDED	NICE TO HAVE

Over the years I have been involved in four different partnerships. While they haven't all been beds of roses, I firmly believe in the value of partnerships for the right situations. Of the four partnerships, three worked out fine and one was a disaster. In my view, the success or failure of the partnership is directly related to the quality of the people involved. A partnership is a marriage, and as such, demands the same degree of care and attention required to nurture and grow a successful marriage. As with a marriage, you are well advised to get to know who you're setting up shop with before signing the agreement.

If you are considering a partnership, tread softly and carry a bullet-proof partnership agreement. Treat your partner with respect, communicate openly, keep your expectations realistic, and be loyal to each other. These things will go a long way towards fostering a long-term, successful partnership.

Partnerships are not appropriate for every situation. The first rule of partnering: If you don't need a partner, don't have one. However, there are a number of good reasons for establishing a partnership, such as:

- To share the workload.
- To attract someone with skills or knowledge you don't already have.
- To bring more money to the table.
- To handle a job or business that is too large for you to manage alone.
- To keep a great person on your team by sharing responsibilities and profits.

Common Causes of Partnership Failure

- Lack of communication.
- Unclear role definition.
- Differing visions or desires for the business.
- Differing values.
- Personality conflicts.
- Business can't afford all or both partners.
- Greed or unrealistic expectations of the business or each other.
- One of the partners does all or most of the work.
- Dishonesty on the part of one or more partners.
- Lack of trust.

Common Misunderstandings About Partnerships

- You don't have to work at keeping the relationship healthy.
- You don't need a signed partnership agreement.
- A partnership lightens the workload. The truth is, with more mouths to feed you will have to work harder in order to bring in more sales. At a minimum, you will have to invest more time communicating.

Key Points About Partnerships

- Partner with someone who complements your skills or who has skills you don't, and clarify your roles.

- Negotiate and sign a partnership agreement–have a lawyer draw it up.

- Assume nothing. Communicate often, honestly and openly.

- Define your vision for the business together, and make any changes to the vision together.

- Before getting into business together, get to know a potential partner well enough to know whether you have compatible values.

- Prior to signing an agreement, ensure that you and any potential partners can effectively resolve conflicts.

- Discuss all of your expectations for each other and the business; ensure the business can afford all or both partners.

- Just as you would before hiring an employee, research the work and investment history to know your potential partner's track record. If there is a history of suing half a dozen previous employers for wrongful dismissal, you probably have a reasonably clear indication of where you will find yourself if the partnership goes sideways.

- Exit of one or more partners can cause business disruption–be sure to include an exit clause in your partnership agreement.

Step 77: Include Lease Agreement(s)

MUST HAVE	RECOMMENDED	NICE TO HAVE

When getting into business, it takes either deep pockets or a lot of courage to sign a lease.

Take a long, hard look at the risk before locking yourself into any business-related lease. I have observed too many bailout applications from failing businesses rife with costly long-term leases. When my own business went down in flames in 1986, I was the proud signatory on iron-clad leases for a few brand new 4 × 4 trucks. If the hair doesn't stand up on the back of your neck when considering a lease, you are either really confident in your business, or not paying attention. Signer beware!

Heads-up for anyone considering locking into a lease for the early stages of business:

1. Lease agreements are typically for a longer period of time than a rental agreement.

2. Leases typically offer lower rates in return for locking you in for a longer period of time.

3. Lease agreements are often easy to get into and very difficult, if not impossible, to get out of.

4. Even when you think you can get out of a lease, troublesome clauses seem to pop out of the paperwork.

5. Lease agreements are usually created by and for the benefit of the lessor rather than the lessee (that would be you).

Be wary of commercial leases that provide the lessor with the option to increase your lease commensurate with your revenue or profit. I recall a case involving a small shop whose lease payments had increased from about $2,000 per month to more than $8,000 because of such a clause.

Step 78: Include Insurance Documents

MUST HAVE	RECOMMENDED	NICE TO HAVE

You don't need to include entire contracts or policies, only the proof of purchase. For example, my liability insurance policy has one page that proves I am insured and provides enough information to satisfy the business plan reader.

Action

Secure a copy of the appropriate insurance documentation and include it in the Appendix.

Link: Download a free Insurance Checklist Worksheet from **www. riskbuster.com/worksheet/59-insurance-checklist**

Tip: Keep your original documents and include copies only in your Appendices, in case readers don't return the originals.

Tip: Get advice from your lawyer and accountant before you sign a lease.

Tip: Prior to signing your lease, be clear as to whether you can make leasehold improvements, and who owns the improvements once they are made.

Tip: If your lease agreement document is hefty, consider providing only the cover and signature page in the Appendix, and state that the full document is available upon request.

Step 79: Develop Your Price List

MUST HAVE	RECOMMENDED	NICE TO HAVE

Include a list of prices for your products and or services.

If your business sells six or fewer products or services, include your price list in the body of your business plan instead. If you are selling a broad range of products or services, you may opt to include your price list here.

Prices are also referred to as unit prices.

Actions

1. Create your price list.

2. Include your price list in the Appendix.

Link: Download a free Price List Worksheet from Macrolink at **www.riskbuster.com/worksheet/60-price-list**

Tip: Consider using a table, which includes your competitor prices and provides a clear view of how you are differentiated from your competition.

Step 80: Gather and Include Price Quotes

MUST HAVE	RECOMMENDED	NICE TO HAVE

Any documentation you gather for this Section will protect you later. For example, it is a healthy thing to get quotes from suppliers in order to keep straight what was promised, when it was said, and by who. There's nothing quite as strong as the written word to quash any discrepancies or arguments that might arise later.

Items that require price quotes might include:

- Product or service suppliers.
- Proposed equipment purchases.
- Owned or leased properties.

Actions

1. Get written prices from as many sources as is appropriate, usually at least three; the only time just one source is suitable is when there *is* only one source.

2. Include only the best source in the Appendix, unless you feel strongly that one or more of the others proves a point.

Tip: Demonstrate wise buying practices by shopping around. If possible, get quotes from at least three different sources.

Tip: Be sure to have providers of the quotes include expiry dates.

Step 81: Get Written Estimates

MUST HAVE	RECOMMENDED	NICE TO HAVE

Obtain independent appraisals or estimates of the value of any large ticket items in your business plan.

Lenders will always view your self-appraisals with a jaundiced eye; it is far more credible to include a written appraisal or estimate from a third party, such as a professional appraiser or some other highly credible firm.

A number of situations might benefit by including an appraisal or estimate, such as:

- Real estate (the most common example).

- When seeking a loan to purchase equipment; it will strengthen your case to include a written estimate from someone known for his or her knowledge about the item.

- When you aspire to use tools or equipment that you already owned as owner's equity or security on a sought-after loan.

Actions

1. Review your assets, capital purchases, and any items you are offering to provide for security.

2. Determine whether the value of any of the items will be questioned by the lenders or potential investors.

3. Select a credible professional and have them do the appraisal, valuation, or assessment.

4. Include the appropriate appraisal documentation in the Appendix.

Step 82: Provide the Right Survey Info

MUST HAVE	RECOMMENDED	NICE TO HAVE

Rarely will you need to include your market surveys in your business plan, but the information will be necessary. The easiest way to do this is by compiling the results to create a summary.

Action

Summarize your market survey information and include it in the Appendix.

Caution: You will not impress anyone by dumping a disorganized pile of paper in this Element. Summaries, tables, and graphics are more effective methods for getting your point across.

Tip: Refer your reader to this Element from the appropriate places in the body of your business plan.

Step 83: Create a Map of Your Market Area

MUST HAVE	RECOMMENDED	NICE TO HAVE

Sometimes a simple map can help readers locate your business in their mind.

Action

Find and include a map of your market area in the Appendix.

Caution: don't include a map just because there is an Appendix for it; determine for yourself whether or not it will enhance the communication process, and leave it out if it's unnecessary.

Tip: Ensure that the document at least matches the level of professionalism represented in the rest of your business plan. For example, clean up any poor quality photocopies.

Tip: If your map can be portrayed in an uncomplicated way on less than half a page, consider placing it directly into the body of your business plan.

Step 84: Include Environmental Information

MUST HAVE	RECOMMENDED	NICE TO HAVE

If you are opening a gas station, you may be scrutinized and regulated by certain government agencies. If your business will impact the environment, you may risk attracting negative publicity from environmental groups or concerned neighbors. For example, if you wish to access funding from government sources, you will be required to complete (or have an expert complete) an environmental assessment impact.

Whatever your business, you must have one eye on the environment and make every effort to protect or manage it in the course of your business. In spite of my disdain for government forms and processes, I would hope you would want to do this anyway—it's just good business.

Readers of your business plan will want to know that you have educated yourself on any environmental issues, and that you have taken every precaution to manage environmental risks.

Action

Gather and store any pertinent environmental information here and refer your reader to it in the relevant parts of the body of your business plan.

Tip: For lengthy documents, summarize the key points and state that the full document is available upon request.

Step 85: Gather Free Publicity

MUST HAVE	RECOMMENDED	NICE TO HAVE

This Appendix is most relevant for existing businesses. Although it's not always practical, you can sometimes create publicity as you work toward starting your business.

Action

Gather and include any published articles or promotional pieces that have been written about you, your business, your products, or your services.

Tip: For articles of more than two pages, consider capturing the highlights and quality quotes. State that the full article is available upon request.

Step 86: Create Promotional Materials

MUST HAVE	RECOMMENDED	NICE TO HAVE

No matter what type of business you choose, at some point you will need to create promotional materials.

Promotional materials can include brochures, flyers, business cards, posters, and various digital outputs. If you have the equipment you might decide to produce your promotional materials yourself; if not, you will need to choose a professional to do it for you. Regardless of whether you use a professional, you should maintain responsibility for the setup, decision making, and quality control. After all, you are the boss.

The following component is adapted from a workshop developed by Carmen Brown for Macrolink Action Plans Inc.

First Considerations

When starting down the path of designing your own promotional materials, ask yourself:

- What do you want to achieve?
- Who is the message aimed at?
- What needs to be said?
- How will you convey this message?

Use the AIDA Format for Creating Promotional Materials. The AIDA format is helpful in creating your marketing piece, whether it is a brochure, poster or flyer. The four parts of AIDA are:

A - Attention (grabber)
How does this flyer capture the consumer's attention?

Example: Headline stating, "African monkey successfully forecasts financials with Macrolink's Biz4Caster™!" Photo showing a monkey towering over a notebook computer, beating it's chest triumphantly.

I - Interest (highlights features)

What keeps the consumer interested in reading?

Example: CD contains ready-to-use business plan and financial templates; don't have to think about the technical; let's you focus on your business.

D - Desire (describes benefits)

What's in it for the consumer?

Example: Start your dream business today with confidence! Saves you valuable time, energy, and money!

A - Action (asks reader to do something)

What is the call to action?

Example: Sale ends Tuesday. Call us while supplies last, at 250-612-9161.

Some Budget Considerations

Listed on the following page are a number of factors that affect the cost of promotional materials. You can use several variables from this information to keep within your budget.

THINGS TO CONSIDER WHEN DEVELOPING PROMOTIONAL MATERIALS		
Factor	*Least Expensive*	*Most Expensive*
Paper weight	20 lb bond white	80 lb cover stock, colored
Paper color	White	Colored
Paper finish	Linen (checker finish), cheapest Laid (line finish), 2nd cheapest	Smooth (cover stock), most expensive
Paper size	8.5" × 11"	17.5" × 23.5" standard size Die cut odd shape paper
Ink colors	One color	Four colors
Number of brochures	More = cheaper per copy at a print shop Fewer = cheaper to print on your home computer	Small-number runs– print-shop setup fees are the same for large runs or small
Layout and design	You create and supply in a compatible format to printer	Setup time at print shop
Proofing	Ensure that text and layout are correct and confirm with printer all the specifics *prior* to printing	Reprint the entire run *after* errors are discovered
Photographs	Provide photographs yourself	Use a professional for top-quality photographs

Promotional Materials Pitfalls to Avoid

Your promotional material is your face in the marketplace. You will want to avoid these common pitfalls:

1. Blurry logos, print, or photographs.

2. Incorrect website address such as *.com* instead of *.net.*

3. Spelling or grammatical errors.

4. Color mismatched to your other marketing materials.

5. Sloppy or inaccurate folding.

6. Much higher cost than anticipated, due mostly to added setup costs.

Be careful not to fall into the trap of assuming that your marketing is finished once you produce promotional materials. Your work is actually just beginning at that point. Professional marketing materials supplement, rather than replace, your marketing efforts. Your strongest marketing technique is to get yourself out into your market and interact with your customers.

Tips for Choosing a Print Shop

1. Get estimates in writing from at least three printers for each job.

2. Determine costs for (a) setup, (b) first printing, and (c) additional printing.

3. Decide if you need quantity, quality, or a combination.

4. Read the fine print before signing a contract, and make sure you understand the language.

5. Never assume anything. Check twice, print once–make sure your product is perfect.

Step 87: Add Product Literature

MUST HAVE	RECOMMENDED	NICE TO HAVE

When selling a product or service provided by a third party or supplier, you should be able to obtain literature, preferably at no cost.

If you are creating your product or service for sale, you will need to create your own literature.

This Element can be a simple printed document or a more expensive output, such as a glossy color brochure printed by professionals.

Product or Service Literature (this step) is similar to Technical Information (see Step 88 on page 258). If having two Elements is potentially confusing to your reader, create one Appendix to hold both. Ultimately it doesn't matter what you call the Appendix, as long as your readers can easily locate what they are looking for.

Product or Service Literature is intended to help the reader visualize what you are selling.

Action

Gather or create any Product or Service Literature and put it into this Element.

Tip: Go easy on the eye candy! Promotional materials can be pretty, but the real meat of your business plan will be of more interest to most readers. Don't be blinded by fancy graphics, fonts, or marketing materials.

Step 88: Add Technical Information

MUST HAVE	RECOMMENDED	NICE TO HAVE

Technical information is most useful when you have a product or service that is complex or not easily understood by your reader. It is preferable to include detailed information such as this in the Appendices, rather than in the body of your business plan.

Some will read it, others won't.

This type of information can often be gathered from suppliers. If you are creating your own product or service, you will need to create your own technical information.

Although Technical Information (this step) is similar to Product or Service Literature (see Step 87 on page 257), it might be written for technicians and have less of a marketing angle. If technicians are your target customers, these two Elements might be the same.

Action

Gather or create any technical information that detail oriented readers will hunger for, and put it into this Element.

Tip: If your technical information outweighs the body of your plan, you're probably getting carried away. Technical information should supplement your plan, not tilt it toward the garbage bin.

Tip: You can get away with far more detail and jargon in the material in this Element than is possible in the body of your business plan. The body of your plan must communicate to a more general audience, while this Element can "talk techie."

Step 89: Explain Any Confusing Terms

MUST HAVE	RECOMMENDED	NICE TO HAVE

Each business has its jargon. Jargon is typically a language that is used within an Industry or business type. One characteristic of jargon is that it may be misunderstood or not understood by those outside the Industry or business, thereby requiring clarification. Use this Element only if absolutely necessary.

Actions

Create a Glossary of Terms for your reader.

1. Reread your business plan.

2. Identify any words that may be confusing to your reader.

3. Make a list of the terms along with explanations or definitions.

4. Place your Glossary of Terms as the last Appendix in your business plan.

Tip: When you see that you have used jargon or a confusing term, search for another way to say the same thing; often there are many ways to communicate thoughts and ideas.

Tip: If your business plan contains only a few confusing words or terms, provide your explanations in the body of your plan or as footnotes.

Craft Your Final Presentation

The purpose of this Section is to create the introductory part of your business plan.

Here are the four Elements in this Section and the corresponding RoadMap™ steps:

BUSINESS PLAN ELEMENT	ROADMAP STEPS
Title Page	90
Executive Summary	91
Table of Contents	92
Confidentiality Statement	93

If you're using a computer and working with the RiskBuster Business Plan Shell™, your Title Page, Table of Contents, and Confidentiality Statement will already be substantially done.

The table on the following page provides a brief description of each Introductory Element.

Link: Download a free RiskBuster Business Plan Shell™ from **www.riskbuster.com/member/member-resources**

Link: Download a copy of the Macrolink Business Plan from **www.riskbuster.com/content/business-plan**

Step 90: Create Your Title Page

MUST HAVE	RECOMMENDED	NICE TO HAVE

The purpose of this Element is to build the cover for your business plan.

The Title Page is one of the finishing touches to your business plan. It should include your company name and logo, and it should be identified as a business plan and include the date, your name, mailing address, phone number and email address—similar to the example in the next chapter.

A few things to note about the Title Page:

- It should look professional.

- It is acceptable to use some graphics, but too many tend to detract from a professional appearance.

- Use a font that is clear and easy to read.

- Include your contact information and business name.

- You might consider adding the name of the agency you are submitting the plan to; for example, add "Prepared for" or "Submitted to."

Link: Download your free bonus copy of the RiskBuster Business Planner™ at **www.riskbuster.com/RiskBusterBook**

Tip: If you're using the Business Plan Shell™, the Title Page is already set up for you.

Tip: When you go online to register and get your free bonus copy of the RiskBuster Business Planner, your access code is daclbo707.

Daclbo707

Step 91: Write Your Executive Summary

MUST HAVE	RECOMMENDED	NICE TO HAVE

The purpose of the Executive Summary is to provide the reader with a brief introduction to you, your business, your plan, and your request. This Element will highlight the important points contained in the business plan. If the Executive Summary is poorly written, the reader may not read the remainder of the business plan.

The Executive Summary is usually the first Element your reader will read, and it is the last Element you will write. It consists mainly of small segments copied or adapted from the main body of your business plan. However, if you wrote your Business Vision (see Step 9 on page 63), and if it is still relatively accurate, you may have already completed the bulk of your Executive Summary.

If your concept has changed significantly from when you wrote the Business Vision, you may find it easier to use the following process to pull together your Executive Summary. Either way, the following table shows the Elements of your Executive Summary and which Elements of your business plan to copy or adapt them from.

Example: Executive Summary

Identity Statement

Macrolink Action Plans Inc. (Macrolink) is a privately held corporation headquartered in Prince George and registered in the Province of British Columbia. Founded in 1987, the business has focused mainly on delivery of training throughout Northern BC. This business plan is the owner's roadmap to reconfigure the business and implement a new marketing strategy for growth. The owner and principal shareholder is Dan Boudreau.

Example: Executive Summary (Continued)

Mission and Vision

Macrolink provides practical, affordable business planning solutions for do-it-yourself entrepreneurs. The vision is to be the resource of choice for entrepreneurs, ensuring customer satisfaction every time.

Description of Products and Services

Each year millions of people get involved in starting businesses. Most of those who successfully navigate the start-up phase will need a business plan. While it may be realistic for well-educated and adequately funded entrepreneurs to create a business plan, many do not have MBAs or deep pockets. Most are taken aback to learn they must write a business plan and are stressed by the realization that they will have to do it themselves. Tragically, many give up in frustration instead of starting their dream business. Macrolink Business Planning products and services empower novices with viable proposals to prove their business case and create a meaningful business plan. Macrolink offers the following products and services:

1. Books for Business Planners
2. Digital Tools for Business Planners
3. Workshops for Business Planners
4. Facilitator Manuals for Business Plan Counselors and Trainers
5. Consulting and Business Plan Coaching

Trends and Objectives

This business plan is built on the following trends and key points:

- It has become more complex to start and operate a business in the past 20 years.
- The book publishing Industry is growing; it has become easier for individuals to participate.
- E-books are the fastest growing area of the book publishing Industry, particularly how-to books.

Example: Executive Summary (Continued)

Trends and Objectives

- The fastest growing types of businesses are non-employer service businesses.

- 300 million or 12.5% of the workforce in 40 countries are involved in entrepreneurial activity.

- In Canada and the United States alone, more than 11,000,000 people are trying to start a business at any given time. The writer estimates 20% will invest a minimum of $50 on business planning products, creating a potential market of $110,000,000 for business planning products.

This business plan includes a strategy to penetrate the market for business planning products and to achieve modest sales targets and success in the marketplace.

Competition and Advantages

There are a number of business planning books and digital products already available in the marketplace, ranging from free to very expensive. Macrolink's success rides on the following competitive advantages:

1. The 99-step RoadMap™ makes business planning manageable for ordinary people.

2. The digital products transform business planning into a safe, fun learning adventure.

3. The workshops offer learners with a practical, interactive way to explore entrepreneurship.

4. The facilitator manuals and materials offer counselors and trainers a fully integrated, ready to use business planning and training system.

5. The consulting and coaching services are affordable, effective, and efficient.

Example: Executive Summary (Continued)

Keys to Success

The keys to Macrolink's success in the marketplace are:

- Successfully penetrating the market by reaching individual entrepreneurs.

- Providing consistently high quality products and services at affordable prices.

- Achieving brand recognition in the minds of the target customers.

- Developing co-marketing alliances with strategic organizations.

- Attracting a major publisher or distributor within three years.

- Keeping overhead to a minimum.

Qualifications

Dan Boudreau, President and CEO, has been involved both as a decision maker and an analyst in projects and business proposals ranging as high as $16 million. As a business owner since 1979, Boudreau has a first-hand understanding of the challenges faced by business owners. Since 1990 he has coached thousands of entrepreneurs through the business planning process. For over 10 years Boudreau has served on the Finance and Lending Committee for Community Futures Development Corporation of Fraser Fort George. This has equipped Boudreau with knowledge and insight into a broad range of small and micro businesses.

Purpose of this Business Plan

This business plan has been created to:

- Serve as the blueprint for Macrolink Action Plans Inc.

- Provide a real living sample business plan to use as a teaching aid.

- Provide benchmarks for evaluating Macrolink's success in the future.

- Communicate the Macrolink Vision to others.

Example: Executive Summary (Continued)

Purpose of this Business Plan

This business plan is scheduled for implementation beginning September 2009, with first year sales forecasted at $128,242, a little over 1% of the total potential market.

The owner is not currently seeking any financing.

Action

The following subsection provides a list of the key topics and a process for creating your Executive Summary.

Process for Creating Your Executive Summary

1. **Identity Statement.** Copy your Identity Statement from Step 31 (see page 116).

2. **Mission Statement.** Copy your Mission Statement from Step 31.

3. **Vision Statement.** Copy your Vision Statement from Step 31.

4. **Brief Description of Products and Services.** Copy or summarize the Description of Products and Services from Step 32 (see page 122). Keep it succinct.

5. **Trends and Gap.** Reread The Industry Element, developed in Step 33 (see page 127). From it, summarize Industry trends and the niche that your business will serve.

6. **Objectives.** Summarize the three most important objectives from the Strategic Plan and Goals Element, developed in Step 35 (see page 132).

7. **Customers.** Write a summary description of your customers from the Profile of Customers Element developed in Step 38 (see page 138).

8. **Competition and Advantages**. Create a succinct paragraph that describes your competitors overall and explains why customers will buy from your business. This comes from the

Competition and Differentiation Element created in Step 39 (see page 141).

9. **Qualifications.** From your The Owner Element developed in Step 34 (see page 130), create one brief paragraph about each owner. Explain why the owner is qualified to make this business a success.

10. **Financial Request or Requirements.** If applicable, review the Financial Section of your Business Plan and briefly explain how much funding you are seeking.

11. **Security.** If applicable, describe what you are prepared to offer the lender for security on your loan.

WORKSHEET: EXECUTIVE SUMMARY	
Topic	*Narrative - Notes*
Identity Statement	
Mission Statement	
Vision Statement	
Brief Description of Products and Services	
Trends and Gaps	
Objectives	
Customers	
Competition and Advantages	
Qualifications	
Financial Request or Requirements	
Security	

Link: Download a free Executive Summary Worksheet from **www. riskbuster.com/worksheet/61-executive-summary**

Step 92: Develop Your Table of Contents

MUST HAVE	RECOMMENDED	NICE TO HAVE

This Element of the business plan provides an easy road map for the reader to quickly locate the various Elements. Your Table of Contents should be similar to the list of Elements (see pages 51 and 52) and contain accurate headings, subheadings and page numbers. Word processing programs have automatic Table of Contents functions that not only ensure that accurate page numbers are referenced but also can be adjusted easily, should your page numbers change.

How to Create a Table of Contents in Microsoft Word™

In Microsoft Word™, the Table of Contents function works with formatting in the body of your document. What this means to your business plan is that all headers you wish to appear in the Table of Contents must be formatted as a header (Header 1, Header 2, etc.). To create a Table of Contents, once you have formatted all headers within the document:

1. Click where you want to insert the Table of Contents.

2. On the **Insert** menu, point to **Reference**, and click **Index and Tables**.

3. Click the **Table of Contents** tab.

4. To use one of the available designs, click a design in the **Formats** box.

5. Select any other Table of Contents options you want.

Link: Download a free copy of the Business Plan Shell™ from **www.riskbuster.com/member/member-resources**

Tip: If you're using the Business Plan Shell™, the Table of Contents is already set up for you.

Step 93: Write Confidentiality and Copyright

MUST HAVE	RECOMMENDED	NICE TO HAVE

Here are sample formats for each of the Confidentiality and Copyright Elements. Adapt each Element to make the wording appropriate for the readers of your Business Plan.

Example: Confidentiality Statement

The reader acknowledges that the information provided by Macrolink Action Plans Inc. in this business plan is confidential; therefore, readers agree not to disclose it without the express written permission of the writer. Other than information that is in the public domain, any disclosure or use of the information by the reader may cause harm or serious damage to Macrolink Action Plans Inc. Upon request, this document is to be returned promptly to Dan Boudreau.

Example: Copyright Statement

Copyright © 2009 Macrolink Action Plans Inc.

All rights reserved. No part of this document may be reproduced or transmitted in any form or by any means now known or to be invented, electronic or mechanical, including photocopying, recording or other information storage or retrieval system, without written permission from Macrolink Action Plans Inc.

Created by: Macrolink Action Plans Inc.
Box 101, Prince George, BC V2L 4R9

Action

Create your Confidentiality and Copyright statements.

Step 94: Evaluate Your Business Plan

MUST HAVE	RECOMMENDED	NICE TO HAVE

The following questions will help you evaluate your business plan.

1. Do you show relevant Industry and business experience?

2. Are you clear as to which products or services the business will sell?

3. Have you confirmed a reliable supply of materials, products, and services?

4. Have you surveyed potential customers to confirm demand?

5. Have you confirmed the number of customers and the size of the market?

6. Are you clear as to why a customer would buy the product or service from this business rather than from the competition?

7. Are there credible pro forma financial projections, and do they show enough headroom (gross profit margin) for the business to survive, pay the bills and make a profit?

8. Have you communicated a clear understanding of the Industry?

9. Have you created a credible marketing plan to get the goods to the customers?

10. Have you carried out both primary and secondary market research?

11. Has the product or service been tested or proven by you or others?

12. Are all product and service prices realistic and competitive?

13. Do you have a clear understanding of your competitors?

14. Have you researched and engaged an accountant, a lawyer, and a bookkeeper?

15. Do you understand the major risks or threats to your business?

16. Have you identified the number and type of staff required?

17. Do you have the knowledge and skills to operate the business?

18. Do the credit checks reveal a positive history for managing finances?

19. Have you completed a detailed cash flow projection for the first 12 months?

20. Have you indicated a reasonable rate of growth for Years Two and Three?

21. Have you proven the business case?

22. Does the plan show that you can get enough money to make the business work?

23. Do the financials show that the business can repay any loans?

24. Are you committing enough personal investment to the business?

25. Is the available security sufficient to attract the amount of funding requested?

26. Have you stated credible sources for the factual and numerical information?

27. Do you or your team have enough capacity to implement this business plan?

28. If you were the lender or investor, would you invest your money in this business?

29. After reading this business plan, is your confidence in it high or low?

30. If you were a prospective customer or client, would you purchase these products or services?

Link: Download a free Business Plan Evaluation Checklist from **www.riskbuster.com/worksheet/62-business-plan-evaluation**

Step 95: Have Others Critique Your Plan

MUST HAVE	RECOMMENDED	NICE TO HAVE

Although this step is parked at the tail end of the RoadMap™, critiquing can begin much earlier in the process. You can do some of your own critiquing, but it is important to have others read and provide feedback.

Action

1. Develop your business plan to draft stage and have at least one person proofread it and make corrections.

2. Select three to five people willing to participate in critiquing your business plan.

3. Make copies of your business plan and distribute them to each person. Ask them to read, make notes, and provide feedback.

4. After an appropriate amount of time, meet with each person or the group to debrief.

5. Incorporate all valuable or useful feedback into your business plan.

Tip: Each ounce of energy you invest in revision will save your reader a pound of effort in attempting to understand your message!

Tip: If you have been working with a team throughout the business planning process, you will have had many opportunities to review and evaluate your business plan.

Step 96: Revise and Rewrite Your Business Plan

MUST HAVE	RECOMMENDED	NICE TO HAVE

The time you invest in revising your document will make the difference between clear and unclear writing.

Allow some time to distance yourself from your writing to help you see it more objectively. Read the draft as a reader, rather than as the writer. Find any mistakes and correct them. Read the document several times. Use the list below as a guide to focus your efforts. Never try to look for all potential problems in one go-through—this process takes time and concentration.

BUSINESS PLAN REVISIONS CHECKLIST	
Item	*Checked*
Write in the third person.	
Maintain accuracy and be concise.	
Be consistent with names and terminology.	
Use an active voice and write positively.	
Minimize jargon and avoid clichés.	
Correct all typos and grammatical errors.	
Create a visual format that is easy to read.	
Use appropriate pictures and diagrams.	
Include your sources for key information.	
Include important detail in the Appendices.	
Refer the reader to related information.	
Ensure numerical information matches text.	
Build a cohesive communication package.	

Link: Download a free Business Plan Revisions Checklist from **www.riskbuster.com/worksheet/63-business-plan-revisions-checklist**

Step 97: Complete Your Application for Financing

MUST HAVE	RECOMMENDED	NICE TO HAVE

A sample application is provided here for your convenience, however, most lending agencies will have their own version, and I recommend using theirs.

Name of Applicant(s):		
Name of Business:		
Trade Name:		
Mailing Address:	Postal Code:	
Street Address:	Postal Code:	
Home:	Work:	Fax:

Amount of Loan Requested: $	Term:
Funds Needed For:	
# of Existing Jobs: FT PT	# of Expected Jobs:

Personal Information

Last Name:	First:	Middle:
Social Insurance or Security No.:	Birth Date (MM/DD/YY)	Home Phone:
Current Address:		Years there:
Previous Address:		Years there:

Current or Last Employer:		Occupation:
Phone:	Years there:	Annual Income: $
Prev. Employer:		Occupation:
Phone:	Years there:	Annual Income: $

Marital Status:	□ Single	□ Married	□ C/L
	□ Separated	□ Divorced	□ Widowed

Last Name:	First:	Middle:
Social Insurance or Security No.:	Birth Date (MM/DD/YY):	

Current or Last Employer:		Occupation:	
Phone:	Yrs there:	Annual Income: $	
Prev. Employer:		Occupation:	
Phone:	Yrs there:	Annual Income: $	

References
(customers or employers only–no family or friends)

Name:	Relationship:
Company:	Phone:
Name:	Relationship:
Company:	Phone:
Name:	Relationship:
Company:	Phone:

Step 98: Write Your Cover Letter

MUST HAVE	RECOMMENDED	NICE TO HAVE

Your business plan is complete and ready to go to the reader. It's time to write your cover letter.

If you have not already done so, research the organization(s) to whom you will provide your business plan and get the accurate names, titles and addresses of the person(s) to whom you will send copies.

The purpose of your cover letter is simply to provide an introduction for the reader to your business plan and to yourself. A healthy cover letter should be no more than four paragraphs, including an introduction to the business plan, an introduction to you, a brief confidentiality and directive paragraph, and a polite conclusion. It should be less than one page; almost no circumstances call for more than one page. Your goal is to have the reader quickly set the cover letter aside and be mentally ready and eager to read your business plan.

Paragraph One: Introduction to Your Business Plan

- Introduce business plan and name of business.
- Write one or two sentences describing the business.
- Explain why the reader is receiving the plan (i.e., to consider for a loan or grant).

Paragraph Two: Introduction of Yourself

- Introduce yourself.
- Write one or two sentences about yourself.
- Tell how your expertise or background qualifies you to own or operate the business.

Paragraph Three: Confidentiality and Direction

- Explain the purpose of providing the business plan to the reader.

- Ask that the reader respect confidentiality; authorize appropriate sharing of the plan.

- If appropriate, ask that the business plan be returned, using a self-addressed, stamped envelope.

Paragraph Four: Conclusion

- If you have deadlines, time restrictions, or expectations, briefly state what they are.

- Thank your reader and close the letter optimistically.

Cover-Letter Pitfalls

- Too wordy.

- Too sketchy.

- Cold or impersonal tone.

- Too much hype.

- Too many fonts or graphics.

- Typos, misspelled words, poor grammar.

- Cleverness.

Cover-Letter Must-Do's

- Be professional and business-like; keep it brief.

- Include a self-addressed, stamped envelope if you would like your business plan returned to you.

- Be neat, clean and no-nonsense.

- Proof for typos, spelling, and grammar.

- Sell your strengths.

Example: Cover Letter

Macrolink Action Plans Inc.
Box 101, Prince George, BC V2L 4R9

January 3, 2009

Dear Mr. Scrooge:

Attached is a copy of a business plan for Macrolink Action Plans Inc. The document has been prepared to prove the business case for a home-based micro-business in Prince George, BC. The business will provide practical and affordable business planning solutions for entrepreneurs who wish to develop their own business plans. The financial projections cover a three-year period beginning in September 2009.

For the past 15 years I have been coaching entrepreneurs to develop their own business plans. Over the last 10 years I have served as a member of the Community Futures Development Corporation Finance and Lending Committee, which provides loans to new and existing businesses in the Prince George area. My background in community economic development and small and micro-business lending qualifies me to operate the business described herein.

The Macrolink Business Plan is a confidential document provided as a part of my application to obtain a loan from your organization. I encourage you to share it with any professionals you consider vital to the decision making process. Once you have finished with it, I ask that you please return the business plan to me, using the enclosed self-addressed, stamped envelope.

Thank you for taking the time to review my business plan.

I look forward to hearing from you soon.

Sincerely

Dan Boudreau
President and CEO

Step 99: Present Your Business Plan

MUST HAVE	RECOMMENDED	NICE TO HAVE

Once you know the purpose of your plan and who the target readers are, you can determine what form it will take.

When it comes to professionalism, go the extra mile. In other words, if you're wondering whether or not to include a cover letter, include it. If you're wondering whether to include color pictures or not, include them. Once you have gone to all the effort to build your business plan, it makes little sense to scrimp on the quality of the final package.

It is also advisable to go the distance with communications when submitting your business plan. For example, you might call the recipient to ask when would be a good time to drop off your plan, and then deliver it personally, if possible.

If your business plan is due by a certain date, be sure to get it to the receiver prior to the deadline and then follow up to ensure the recipient received your package. If possible, allow yourself enough time to resubmit the plan if the first copy was not received.

Pay attention to detail. Did the bank or institution request more than one copy? In addition to the hard copy(s), did the receiver request a digital copy on disk or via email? What supporting material was requested? Follow up to assure them that you are available to answer questions, clarify any unclear points or provide further information. Thank the receiver for the opportunity to present your plan.

1. Business Plan for You–the First Customer

The business plan you create for yourself will be the longest version. It will include an Executive Summary, all the narrative and Financial Elements you've created and all the supporting documents in the Appendices. Create one cohesive, bound document that can be easily replicated. Ideally, weave the entire business plan into one digital file as well. This might entail scanning some of the stray supporting documents in order to insert them into your main business plan file. I prefer to use the popular .pdf file format, which makes it easy to print, email, or publish at internal or external websites. The idea is to make it easy for the reader to receive, to navigate, and to reproduce for committee members.

Once you've created your full business plan, you have the raw material to easily create different presentations for a variety of applications. For some situations it may be appropriate to use the full business plan, while for others it will suffice to use only the Executive Summary or certain Elements of your plan. Although most of your modifications will be in the cover letter and the Executive Summary, here are some tips for presenting your business plan to different audiences:

2. Business Plan for Gatekeepers

Most gatekeepers will want a copy of your completed business plan. If you've effectively distilled your market research to a succinct narrative in the body of your business plan, it should meet the needs of most gatekeepers. The key to effective presenting for this audience is to *ask* which Elements they want included.

As an analyst, I prefer to receive both a hard copy and a digital copy of the business plan. The digital file enables me to copy and paste to create my presentation to the decision makers.

3. Business Plan for Your Banker

Bankers are financial people. The presentation you create for your banker might include the Executive Summary, Assumptions, Sales Forecast, Cash Flow Forecast, Projected Income Statement, and Pro Forma Balance Sheet. An option is to attach your full business plan as an Appendix to your presentation; that way, your banker will have the option of digging deeper when desired.

4. Business Plan for Your Employees

The scope of the business plan you present for employees will be in part guided by your philosophy on how much employees should know about the inner workings of your business. To present to employees in the past, I have used the narrative portion of the business plan plus the 3-year sales forecast, but I have excluded the entire Financial Section, Historical Financial Statements, and Appendices.

5. Business Plan for Investors

In developing your presentation for investors, keep in mind what is most important to the reader. Investors will need to know whether you are seeking debt or equity financing, and they will want to know such items as the potential return on their investment, risk and mitigation, security and exit strategies.

6. Executive Summary

Your Executive Summary, dealt with in detail in Step 91 (see page 263), can be used as a communication tool. With minimal adjustments, it can be used to introduce your business to various audiences. It can be used as a component of presentations, an addition to proposals, or as a reminder to internal stakeholders. Your Executive Summary provides most of the information needed to create a prospectus, which is a legal document that businesses use to describe the securities they are offering for participants and buyers.

7. A One-Page Business Plan

The market research, the planning process, and the full written business plan are necessary educational and management tools. However, once you get thoroughly immersed in running your business it is practical to have a simple one-page summary of the main points from your business plan. This document should be designed to meet your needs and might include the Vision, Mission, Strategic Plan, Goals, Marketing Action Plan, Sales Targets and Financial Goals. The purpose of the one-page plan is to keep your key information visible as a constant reminder and guide for your day to day business decisions.

8. Your Elevator Pitch

An elevator pitch is a brief introduction of your business idea. The term is often used in the context of an entrepreneur pitching an idea to an angel investor or venture capitalist to receive funding. It can be delivered in the time span of an elevator ride. It might be as long as thirty seconds or 100 to 150 words.

Suggested Reading

Allen, James. *As a Man Thinketh.* Marina del Rey, California: DeVorss & Company.

Alreck, Pamela L., & Settle, Robert B. *The Survey Research Handbook.* Columbus, Ohio: Irwin/McGraw-Hill, 1995.

Beinhocker, Eric D. *The Origin of Wealth: Evolution, Complexity, and the Radical Remaking of Economics and What It Means for Business and Society,* 1st ed. Boston, Massachusetts: Harvard Business School Publishing, 2007.

Chilton, David Barr. *The Wealthy Barber,* 1st ed. Toronto, Ontario: Stoddart Publishing Co. Limited, 1995.

Clason, George S. *The Richest Man in Babylon.* New York, New York: New American Library, Penguin Putnam Inc., 1955, 1988.

Comm, Joel. *Twitter Power,* 1st ed.

United States of America: John Wiley & Sons, Inc. 2009.

Covey, Stephen R. *The 7 Habits of Highly Effective People,* 1st Fireside ed. New York, New York: Fireside, 1990.

Cyr, Donald, & Gray, Douglas. *Marketing Your Product,* 3rd ed. Bellingham, Washington: Self-Counsel Press Ltd. 1998.

Doman, Don, Dennison, Dell, & Doman, Margaret. *Market Research Made Easy,* 2nd ed. USA and Canada: International Self-Counsel Press Ltd., 2002.

Dominguez, Joe, & Robin, Vicki. *Your Money or Your Life,* 1st ed. New York, New York: Penguin Books, 1992.

Doyle, Denzil J. *Making Technology Happen,* 5th ed. Ottawa, Ontario: Doyletech Corporation, 2001.

Dyer, Wayne W. *You'll See It When You Believe It,* 1st Avon Books Printing. New York, New York: Avon Books, 1990.

Finkel, David, & Kennedy, Diane. *The Maui Millionaires for Business,* 1st ed.

United States of America: John Wiley & Sons, Inc. 2008.

Friedman, Thomas L. *The World Is Flat,* 1st ed. New York, New York: Farrar, Straus and Giroux, 2005.

Fulghum, Robert. *All I Really Need to Know I Learned in Kindergarten,* 1st Ballantine ed. New York, New York: Ballantine Books, 1989.

Gerber, Michael E. *The E Myth Revisited,* 1st ed. New York, New York: HarperCollins Publishers, Inc., 1995.

Godin, Seth. *The Meatball Sundae,* 1st ed. New York, New York: Penguin Group, 2007.

Godin, Seth. *Purple Cow,* 1st ed. New York, New York: Penguin Group, 2002.

Hawken, Paul. *The Ecology of Commerce,* 1st ed. New York, New York: HarperCollins Publishers, 1993.

Hawken, Paul. *Growing a Business,* 1st ed. New York, New York: Fireside, 1988.

Hill, Napoleon. *Think and Grow Rich,* 1st Ballantyne Books ed. New York, New York: Ballantyne Books, 1990.

Kennedy, Dan, & Scrob, Robert, & Regnerus, Bob. *The Official Get Rich Guide to Information Marketing,* 1st ed.

Canada: Entrepreneur Media Inc. 2007.

Kiyosaki, Robert T. *Rich Dad, Poor Dad.* 1st ed. New York, New York: Warner Books, Inc., 1998.

Levinson, Jay Conrad. *Guerrilla Marketing,* 1st ed. Boston, Massachusetts: Houghton Mifflin Company, 1984.

Levinson, Jay Conrad. *Guerrilla Marketing Weapons,* 1st ed. New York, New York: Penguin Group, 1990.

McCormack, Mark H. *What They Don't Teach You at Harvard Business School*, 1ˢᵗ ed. New York, New York: Bantam Books, Inc., 1986.

Peters, Thomas J., & Waterman, Jr., Robert H. *In Search of Excellence*, 1ˢᵗ ed. New York, New York: Warner Books, Inc., 1982.

Peterson, Mark A. *The Complete Entrepreneur*, 1ˢᵗ ed. Hauppauge, New York: Barron's Educational Series, Inc., 1996.

Ries, Al, & Trout, Jack. *Marketing Warfare*, 1ˢᵗ ed. New York, New York: McGraw-Hill, 1986.

Ries, Al, & Trout, Jack. *The 22 Immutable Laws of Marketing*, 1ˢᵗ ed. New York, New York: HarperCollins Publishers, 1994.

Silver, Yanik. *Moonlighting on the Internet*, 1ˢᵗ ed.

Canada: Entrepreneur Media Inc. 2008.

Sirolli, Ernesto. *Ripples from the Zambezi: Passion, Entrepreneurship, and the Rebirth of Local Economies*, 1ˢᵗ ed. Murdoch, Western Australia: Institute for Science and Technology Policy, Murdock University, 1995.

Skrob, Robert, & Regnerus, Bob. *The Official Get Rich Guide to Information Marketing on the Internet*, 1ˢᵗ ed.

Canada: Entrepreneur Media Inc. 2008.

Sun Tzu. *The Art of War.* New York, New York: Oxford University Press, 1971.

Index

B

Band Council Resolution (BCR), 234
bank accounts, 12–13
bankers, 176, 217, 232, 281
benefits
  describing, 254
  selling, 124–125
biography, owner, 130–131, 229, 268
Biz4Caster™
  cash flow forecasts, 201
  downloadable version, 51
  financial section, 51, 188
  income statements, 208
  in planning steps, 49–51
  pricing worksheet, 156
Bizplan Builder software, 142
blogs, 25–26
board of directors, 233
bookkeepers, 177–178
boolean web searches, 24–25
break-even analysis, 211–212
Break Even Analysis Worksheet, 212
break-even pricing, 152. *See also*
  prices and pricing strategy
Brown, Carmen, 253
Building a Business Planning Team
  Worksheet, 10
burnout and fatigue, 169
business case, proving, 60–62,
  111–114
business concept section, 115–133
  business description, 116–121
  Elements checklists, 115, 116
  features customers want, 124–125
  industry description, 127–129
  owner biography, 130–131, 229, 268
  products and services, 122–126
  selling the benefits, 124–125
  strategic plan and goals, 115, 132–
    133, 182
  worksheets, 116, 123, 126, 132–133
business counseling services, 143

business description, 116–121
Business Element, 116–121
  business description, 119
  identity statement, 117
  legal considerations, 119–120
  mission statement, 118, 133
  regulatory considerations, 119–120
  vision statements, 49, 59, 118, 133,
    263
  writing process, 116
business ideas
  searches for, 26–28
  transition to action, 45–46
Business Plan Elements Checklist, 116
Business Plan Evaluation Checklist,
  272
Business Planner
  access code, 262
  Checklist, 13, 51
Business Planning Goals Worksheet,
  55
business planning primer, 1–44.
  See also business plans; finances;
  websites
  deal breakers, 16–17
  financing, 31–33
  gatekeepers, 34–35
  goal setting, 3
  Internet, 23–30
  names for businesses, 21–22
  readiness evaluation, 8
  team building, 9–10
  technical skills, 7–8
  time management, 2, 11
  types of businesses, 18–20
  worksheets, 2, 3, 4, 5, 8, 10
  writing skills, 6
Business Plan Pro software, 142
Business Plan Revisions Checklist,
  274
business plans, 45–62. *See also*
  Business Plan Shell™; Macrolink
  Business Plan; RoadMap™

290

computers, website and technology protection, 169
confidentiality agreements, 232
consulting services, 142
contracts
in appendices, 240
with human resource suppliers, 166
labor, 166, 179
copyright
for business names, 22
in presentation statements, 270
as protection, 170
cost of goods sold (COGS), 152, 156, 196–197, 208
Cost of Goods Sold Worksheet, 197
cover letter, presentation, 277–279
outline of, 277–278
pitfalls to avoid, 278
success tips, 278
credit
long-term, 32
ratings, 17
short-term, 31, 33
customers
marketing section description, 138–140
in market research, 92, 110
market surveys, 101, 108, 173
prioritization and targeting of, 99–100, 139
products and services, 124–125
worksheets, 92, 138

D

databases
of topical media, 27, 57
of trade publications, 57
deal breakers, 16–17
debt, 172
descriptors checklist, resumé, 225, 228

diagrams, 38
differentiation from competitors, 96–97, 141–144, 246
directories, web, 25
disputes, 168
document storage, 54
domain names for websites, 22, 23–24, 28
Draft Description of Customers Worksheet, 92

E

Ebay keywords website, 26
Elements, 47–48. *See also specific business plan aspects*
elevator pitch, 283
email skills, 7
embassy websites, 30
employees, 174–175, 179–181, 281–282
environmental assessment impact, 251
equipment and methods, 164–165
Equipment and Methods Worksheet, 165
equity, 71, 213, 217, 219, 248
equity financing, 32, 282
executive summary, presentation, 263–268, 282
Executive Summary Worksheet, 268
existing businesses
buying of, 20, 232
historical financials, 232
Internet searches for, 23–24
expiration dates, price quotes, 247
Explaining Your Projections Worksheet, 191–193
e-zines, 26

Google™, 26, 29
government-owned organizations, 234
guarantees, 147

H

health and safety, 168
hiring criteria, 174
historical financials for existing
businesses, 232
Hong Kong Export Credit
Insurance Corporation website, 30
human resource suppliers, 166

I

ideas. *See* business ideas
identity statements, 117
income statements, 156, 206–210,
232
industry
business concept description, 127–129
classification system, 84–85
Key Industry Statements Worksheet,
85
knowledge of, 57
market research description, 84–90
websites, 30
inspiration lists, 3
insurance, 173, 245
Insurance Checklist Worksheet, 245
intangible properties, 170
International Franchise Association,
19
international Internet websites, 30
Internet, 23–30. *See also* websites
basic computer skills, 7
boolean web searches, 24–25
existing business searches, 23–24
international resources, 30
keyword searches, 24–25
market research, 26–28

name research, 22
resources, 25–28
RSS feeds, 26, 29
search engines, 25, 28–29, 52
surveys, 103, 173
Internet Explorer™, 52
Internet surveys, 103, 173
Investment Comparison Worksheet,
114
investors, xix, 5, 17, 221, 224, 248,
282

J

Japanese External Trade
Organization website, 30
jargon, 259
job descriptions, 174
job experience, 102
journals, 58

K

Key Industry Statements Worksheet,
85

L

labor contracts, 166, 179
labor projections, 181, 198, 208
Labor Projections Worksheet, 181,
208
labor requirements, 179–181
laws and regulations, 119–120, 171
lawsuits, 17, 20, 169
lawyers, 22, 170, 177, 232, 240,
243, 245
leases, 163, 213, 244, 245, 247
legal considerations. *See also* lawyers
board of directors, 234
business structures, 21–22
disputes, 168

lawyers, 22, 170, 177, 232, 240, 243, 245
  meetings with, 175
  selection of, 176–178
Professional Services Worksheet, 178
Profile of Customers Worksheet, 138
profit and loss statements, 206–210
Pro Forma Balance Sheet Worksheet, 213–215
Projected Income Statement Worksheet, 209, 210
Projected Income Summary Worksheet, 209
Projected Labor Summary Worksheet, 198
projections. *See also* forecasts
  explanation of, 191–193
  income statements, 156, 206–210, 232
  labor, 181, 198, 208
  worksheets, 181, 191–193, 198, 209–210
promotional materials
  AIDA format for creating, 253–254
  choosing print shops, 256
  cost factors, 254–255
  pitfalls to avoid, 256
promotion and advertising, 149–151, 159, 252
prospectus, 282
Proving Your Business Case Worksheet, 60, 111
publicity, 252
purposeful action, 2

Q

questionnaires, market surveys, 104–107, 109

R

rainy-day fund, 202
references

letters from, 236–237
list of, 235
repairs, 147
Resumé for Entrepreneurs Worksheet, 229
resumés, 224–229
  action words and strong descriptors, 224–225, 228
  length of, 229
  Owner Element and, 229
  parts of, 226
  worksheets, 227, 229
return on investment (ROI), 113–114
Return on Investment (ROI) Worksheet, 113–114
RiskBuster™. *See also* Biz4Caster™; Business Plan Shell™; Macrolink Business Plan; RoadMap™; worksheets
  Business Planner access code, 262
  Business Planner Checklist, 13
  Financial Forecast, 51
  Market Research Springboard, 28
  website, 51
RiskBuster™ Newsletter, 42
RiskBuster Market Research SpringBoard, 28
risk identification and control, 168–173
  bad debts, 172
  cash flow shortfalls, 172, 197
  competitor reactions, 171
  computers, website and technology, 169
  copyright protection, 170
  disputes, 168
  facilities and equipment, 169
  fatigue and burnout, 169
  fire and emergency, 169
  health and safety, 168
  intangible properties, 170
  laws and regulations, 171
  lawsuits or fines, 169

telephone surveys, 103
terminology, explanation of, 259
text boxes, presentation documents, 41
Threats and Mitigation Worksheet, 173
timelines, 55, 132–133, 183
time management
  exceeding expectations, 11
  in goal setting, 2, 49–50
title pages, presentation, 261, 262
tools, 52. *See also specific software*
Total Market Potential, 195
trade
  associations, 57
  Internet research, 30
  NAFTA, 84
  publications, 57, 83
trademarks
  name, 22
  as protection, 170
typing tutorial software, 8

U

units, 67–68, 70
URL (Uniform Resource Locator), 23
Use and Source of Funds
  Worksheet, 220

V

vision statements, 49, 59, 118, 133, 263
Vivísimo search engine, 29

W

wages, 174–175, 180
web browsers, 52
websites
  About.com, 26

archives, 25
Canadian Franchise Association, 19
census information, 28, 85, 99
Commerce Dept., U.S., 30
domain names, 22, 23–24, 28
Ebay keywords, 26
embassies, 30
e-zines, 26
FAQs, 29
Google™ research sites, 26, 29
Hong Kong Export Credit Insurance
  Corporation, 30
industry information, 30
International Franchise Association, 19
international research, 30
Japanese External Trade
  Organization, 30
listservs, 29
market research, 26–28
MediaFinder.com, 27, 57
message boards, 25, 29, 103
newsgroups, 25, 29
OpenOffice.org, 8
RiskBuster.com, xix
risk control of, 169
RSS feeds, 29
Statistics Canada, 85
Surveymonkey.com, 173
trade leads, 30
URL (Uniform Resource Locator), 23
Vivísimo search engine, 29
Yahoo Answers, 27
Zoomerang.com, 173
What's In It For You Worksheet, 5
wordprocessing, 7–8, 52
worksheets
  Action Planning, 56
  Advertising and Promotion Plan
    Checklist, 151
  Appendices, 65
  Appendices Goals, 223
  Assessing What You've Learned, 94
  Assumptions, 71
  Break Even Analysis, 212
  Building a Business Planning Team, 10

Dan Boudreau Biography

Dan Boudreau has devoted the last 20 years to coaching and mentoring regular folks into the captivating world of business. He authors and facilitates lively, transformative workshops on the topics of entrepreneurship, business planning, and training for trainers. He has inspired thousands of entrepreneurs to become successful business owners and leaders.

Launching into his first venture in 1980 with barely enough knowledge to fill the back of a beer cap, he has embraced (and survived) the wide spectrum of business ownership, from single owner home-based enterprises to ventures employing more than 300 workers.

Dan's top life essentials are: laughing, loving, and learning. Armed with the business planning process as a teaching tool, he empowers ordinary women and men to create the financial stability and lifestyle they dream of. He is most proud of being acknowledged and appreciated by peers and friends for his ability to bring entrepreneurial ideas to fruition with a nod towards his warm, engaging personable style.

In 2006, Dan bundled his knowledge (and bruises) into his first book, Business Plan or BUST! In writing the book, he combined his practical experience as a business owner with his expertise as a lender for an economic development agency, and tossed in his unique brand of wit. The end result: A refreshing perspective and no-nonsense style that makes the time-worn topic of business planning easy, fast and fun!

When Dan takes those occasional days off from navigating the business world you might find him stuffed into a floating toothpaste tube sometimes referred to as a kayak (rarely right side up), or perhaps coaxing disturbing sounds from his guitar. From botched attempts to outsmart fish in the rivers of northern British Columbia to flopping around in the waves or practicing applied inertia on just about any tropical beach… his ultimate enjoyment almost always incorporates fresh air, clean water, and sandy beaches.

You can read Dan's bi-weekly practical business planning articles at his blog www.riskbuster.com/blog.

BUY A SHARE OF THE FUTURE IN YOUR COMMUNITY

These certificates make great holiday, graduation and birthday gifts that can be personalized with the recipient's name. The cost of one S.H.A.R.E. or one square foot is $54.17. The personalized certificate is suitable for framing and will state the number of shares purchased and the amount of each share, as well as the recipient's name. The home that you participate in "building" will last for many years and will continue to grow in value.

Here is a sample SHARE certificate:

THIS CERTIFIES THAT

YOUR NAME HERE

HAS INVESTED IN A HOME FOR A DESERVING FAMILY

1985-2005

TWENTY YEARS OF BUILDING FUTURES IN OUR COMMUNITY ONE HOME AT A TIME

1200 SQUARE FOOT HOUSE @ $65,000 = $54.17 PER SQUARE FOOT
This certificate represents a tax deductible donation. It has no cash value.

YES, I WOULD LIKE TO HELP!

I support the work that Habitat for Humanity does and I want to be part of the excitement! As a donor, I will receive periodic updates on your construction activities but, more importantly, I know my gift will help a family in our community realize the dream of homeownership. **I would like to SHARE in your efforts against substandard housing in my community!** *(Please print below)*

PLEASE SEND ME _____ SHARES at $54.17 EACH = $ $_____

In Honor Of: _____

Occasion: (Circle One)   HOLIDAY   BIRTHDAY   ANNIVERSARY

      OTHER: _____

Address of Recipient: _____

Gift From: _____   *Donor Address:* _____

Donor Email: _____

I AM ENCLOSING A CHECK FOR $ $_____ PAYABLE TO HABITAT FOR HUMANITY OR PLEASE CHARGE MY VISA OR MASTERCARD *(CIRCLE ONE)*

Card Number _____ Expiration Date: _____

Name as it appears on Credit Card _____ Charge Amount $ _____

Signature _____

Billing Address _____

Telephone # Day _____ Eve _____

PLEASE NOTE: Your contribution is tax-deductible to the fullest extent allowed by law.
Habitat for Humanity • P.O. Box 1443 • Newport News, VA 23601 • 757-596-5553
www.HelpHabitatforHumanity.org